ANGELA YURIKO SMITH

How To Be an Authortunist

AUTHORTUNITIES

Contents

III   A Few Tools

A Note From the Author

Authortunist. / (au̯.tʰor.tjuːˈnɪst) / noun. A writer who skillfully adapts their actions, responses, and creative strategies to seize opportunities within the publishing world, adapting to trends, market shifts, and evolving circumstances in the literary landscape.

Welcome to my toolkit.

What follows is a collection of essays and workshops I've written over the course of my fiction and nonfiction career that has spanned three decades. I've organized these essays into chapters and I'm trying to pass the whole lot off as a book. Reuse, reduce and recycle are good for writers as well as the planet.

I have shared my favorite productivity hacks, tools and tricks along with some predictions:

Second Life, my favorite virtual world, is going to be available as a mobile app in 2024, I hear. I predict that will finally be the boost this platform needs to be adopted into the mainstream. I talk a lot about how to use Second Life as an easy, free tool with the potential to reach thousands of readers. I share many details on this in the Building Sales section.

As I prepare to publish this, Amazon's KDP Virtual Voice Beta program has just begun, and I've tested it out on five books so far. This will be a game changer for all the smaller writers that can't afford the high cost of audiobook production. It isn't AI voice production, but pretty tolerable Text To Speech. Basically, a synthetic voice reads your words.

No, it's not as wonderful as a human narrator, but human narrators are also out of my price range. If you are listening to this as an audiobook, you are most likely listening to KDP's Virtual Voice. I like to think of it as my voice if I were a robot.

If you read to the end of this book and want even more author opportunities sent to you weekly, please join my *Authortunities* mailing list full of paying submissions, contests, networking, classes, grants, scholarships plus a smattering of industry news... all for free.

Just visit authortunities.substack.com.

Authortunities. / (aʊ.tʰor.tjuːnɪtiz) / noun. A portmanteau of "author" and "opportunities," referring to the various chances, prospects, and avenues available to writers for advancing their craft, publishing their work, and achieving success in the literary world. This term encompasses a range of possibilities, from traditional and self-publishing routes to networking, workshops, and other resources that aid in the development and promotion of an author's work. Also, the title of Angela Yuriko Smith's weekly newsletter full of author opportunities.

I

Building Story

The following section covers my notes gathered from over a decade on how to create successful fiction from the blank page to The End. Starting with fundamentals such as the motivations to write (clarifying this early in a career fast tracks success) to building an intricate plot outline that works without headaches. As I find new information, I share it in my weekly newsletter, Authortunities, which is free to read at authortunities.substack.com.

Much of this was compiled from workshops I've taught. I hope you find it useful.

1

Who I Am & Why I Wrote This

I can give you a boring list of accomplishments, but the most important thing I want you to know is that I'm a lover of books and writing from early on. That's all that really matters. I can't remember a time when I wasn't aware of words. I discovered they could change my world early on. Over the span of my days, they have nourished me, sustained me and saved my life. They have fed my children, got me out of trouble and were my weapon of choice when I needed to defend. Every time I came across a closed door, words proved to be the key I needed to open it.

So that sums up both who I am, and why I wrote this book. I'm a writer and want to share the potential power of it. Words, knowledge and love all share the same kind of magic. The more you share them, the more they come back to you in rewards. I could give all my words away, everyday for the rest of my life and I would still find myself with a galaxy of them to spare.

There are other, less important details about me you might care about. I've shared those at the end of this so anyone curious is welcome to read that later. This place at the beginning is reserved for us to meet, which we just did. I'm happy you're here.

Beginnings are sacred. Here we start a journey together, author and reader. But if you are here, you are most likely not just any reader. You are an author-reader. We are of like mind. You know how powerful story can be, and you want to hone your skills and wield that power.

I hope you find something here that will magnify that power.

2

Why Do You Write?

I t's my least favorite part of the writing process—the moment when I step back, look at what I'm working on and wonder what the heck I was thinking. It's at this moment that any work of art is in the most danger. It's when the creator decides if a project moves on to editing or hits the dustbin.

Stephen King had it when he tossed his original manuscript of *Carrie* into the garbage. We all have moments of self-doubt. It's easy to give up and scrap the whole mess... or prepare ahead of time and reduce the anguish.

KNOW WHY BEFORE YOU TRY

Before you ever set pen to paper and fingers to keyboard, you can head off the terrible moment of doubt by being honest with yourself. It's important to know why you want to write before you commit to it. The good news is there are no wrong answers. The bad news is it can be hard to be honest about our motives to create. Just remember there are no wrong answers and be transparent. If we can't be truthful with ourselves we might have bigger things to work on.

5 REASONS WE WRITE

1. **To make money and be famous.** This is probably the most disparaged motivation for writing but it's a valid one. There is nothing wrong with making a living or getting accolades from what bounces around in your head. If this is your goal as a writer, treat your writing as a commodity. Research markets and trends, find the most lucrative and focus all your efforts there. Money doesn't come without marketing, so make plans for what you will write, and then how you're going to sell it.

2. **To sell yourself and your business.** It's easier to be published now than at any other point in history, but having a published book is still impressive and sets an author up as an expert. Whether you are writing fiction or fact, writing a book can validate you as a thought leader in your field of expertise. James Herriot wrote warm and fuzzy stories about animals as a rural veterinarian. What better advertisement for a veterinarian than heart-warming stories about animals? It's no coincidence he ran a thriving practice until he retired in 1989 at 73 even though he published under a pen name. His veterinarian practice is still in business today.

3. **To teach and inspire.** An altruistic motive, another reason to write is to share knowledge for the betterment of people-kind. A good story can ignite a revolution and change minds… hopefully for the better. Role models are important but not everyone has the blessing to grow up with positive influences in their life. Luckily, those who don't have a flesh and blood inspiration can almost always access the pixel and ink variety. Providing that guidance is a rewarding and precious responsibility.

4. **To entertain and amuse.** Just as noble is the desire to simply entertain. Sometimes people just need a little relief from the daily grind of reality. I learned this during the pandemic when I met a tiny, elderly woman returning a stack of pulp romance novels at the library. "Thank goodness these stories give me something to look forward to or I think I'd just give up" she told me. Not every story needs to change the world. Sometimes just changing one person's world makes all the difference.

5. **Because you are compelled.** I think this is possibly the most difficult to justify. Some writers write because they can't imagine doing anything

else. If they never make a penny, get any recognition or even have a single reader they will still write. Receiving some love for their work makes them happy, but if they were alone in a cave using charcoal and animal skin, they would still be scribbling.

KNOWING WHY IS KNOWING WHAT, WHERE AND WHO

Anyone who thinks the *why* they write doesn't matter is doing an injustice to their self. The *why* is at the heart of everything and can be the difference between fulfillment or frustration. When you know why you want to write it helps you understand what to write, where to release it and for who.

As an example, a lawyer who wants to publish a book to set themselves up as a leader in their industry probably won't benefit from publishing a romance novel unless they specialize in divorce proceedings. But what if their motivation isn't to supercharge their legal practice but to entertain? Then by all means, turn up the steam and let the broken hearts shatter.

Knowing *why* you want to write helps you to streamline your career and avoid the terrible moment of realizing you just spent a good deal of time and energy on something that will not get you where you need to go.

THERE CAN BE MORE THAN ONE

Just remember that why you want to write can change over time and from project to project, and often there is a blend of motivations rather than just one reason. In the case of the lawyer above, what if they wanted to establish themselves as an industry leader and entertain? Then writing thriller novels might be a satisfying option. What if they wanted to be an industry leader and inspire? Nonfiction about criminal redemption might be a good choice. The divorce lawyer might write about relationship topics.

Whatever your motivation, understanding the why will help you know where you want to go with your story. If your intention is to make an income, you'll need to research what genres are selling and where. Paranormal romance seems to do well with younger, female readers and many of them use serial fiction apps like Radish, Wattpad and Webnovel. For those already self-publishing with KDP there is now Kindle Vella to explore. As I get ready to publish this in January of 2024, KDP has just announced the Audiobooks with Virtual Voice Beta.

If your aim is to get a message out, you might want to focus on a blog or ebooks you can distribute free. If you want fame with your fortune, understand the price. You will need effective marketing and a professional, polished product. If this is a one-time bucket list item then perhaps sinking money into your work to get pretty formatting and art is fine. If you are trying to forge a career as an author-preneur, every penny counts and you best barter or teach yourself. There are no wrong answers, but in this case ignorance is not bliss.

KNOWING IS GLOWING

Knowing why you write is the foundation you need to establish for a rewarding career, regardless of motives. And what does a successful writing career look like? If you know *why* you write, it looks exactly like that. Writers that constantly chase trends without knowing why often burn themselves out. Disappointment is their reward.

If you are happy with writing a few stories for the grand kids, don't let anyone make you feel like you aren't a success when you achieve that. At the same time, if your goal is fame and fortune, understand that you are going to work hard, sacrifice much and demolish your comfort zones to get there. You can achieve whatever you want for your work if you know what you are trying to achieve and then take steps to do that.

YOUR TAKEAWAY TASK

This week, take some time to evaluate your motives as a creator. Think of role models and people that inspire you. Try to pinpoint the elements you want to emulate. Why are they a success in your eyes? Chances are, that's what you want. If you could achieve your goal any other way, would you?

3

You Are the Secret Plot Twist

According to polls, more than 80 percent of Americans say they would like to be an author. In 2013, Forbes reported there were "somewhere between 600,000 and 1,000,000 books published every year in the US alone" and they estimate more than half were self published. That was in the early days of the self publishing boom and those numbers have only gone up since. It's clear, there is no shortage of stories in the world and, as the saying goes, there is nothing new under the sun.

This is some heavy information for any author to digest. The weight of it hit me a few years ago during the pandemic. I had a part-time job at one of the largest libraries in Kansas City. We were closed to the public but still in operation thanks to a drive-thru window. Outside the line never stopped as people looked to books for comfort and information. Inside was quiet and dark… a lovely, book lined mausoleum.

NOTHING NEW UNDER THE SUN

During one of my breaks I prowled the dark and deserted shelves, relishing the solitude. The shelves stretched into the shadows. *So many books,* I thought. *Who am I to add even one more?* It was humbling to see thousands of authors lined up on the shelves, the majority of them highly successful. Why did my stories belong among them?

It's enough to make an author put down the pen. The realization wasn't enough to make me quit but it did prompt some solid pondering. Lucky for me, I was pre-armed with some keen insight from my friend and mentor Bryan Thao Worra. Early in my fiction career Bryan had looked over my work. He had one question: where was the *me* in my stories?

At the time, I was writing classic horror with Gothic themes. My work didn't stand out and I didn't know why. I'd bump up the horror and graphic elements... but they were still well edited yawns. Bryan pointed out that I was part Asian and I love tech science. Why didn't I ever use that in my work? The stories I'd written so far could have been written by anyone. Where were the stories that could only be written by me?

YOU MAKE YOUR STORY UNIQUE

To date, that was the best advice I ever got as a writer. My stories were all what I *thought* readers wanted because I'd read these types of stories hundreds of times. That should have been my clue not to write them. We've all read those stories hundreds of times. Why kill another tree for old news?

I'd done a good job keeping my personal quirks out of my work and had created perfectly bland stories. My fiction was just rehashed regurgitation of what I had read before—literary Frankensteins.

Around that time I had an opportunity to submit a story. It was a perfect opportunity to try what Bryan suggested. I had to rush after another deadline, but I managed to come up with an odd tale about being a blended race, generational envy, and the cost of authenticity. Turns out, Bryan's advice was spot on. "Vanilla Rice" was my first professional fiction sale, my breakout story and has been printed three times since.

Every book it appeared in has won or been nominated for high level awards including the Bram Stoker, Shirley Jackson and the Alberta Book Publishing Award for Best Speculative Fiction of the Year. Since the success of that story I look at every story I write through my own perspective... and I've published every story since. Even the rewrites of my old, bland regurgitations have found love when I added the authentic me.

This is what kept me writing that day when I stood alone in a dark library and realized how many excellent stories already existed in the world. Yes, there are "somewhere between 600,000 and 1,000,000 books published every year in the US alone" but there is only one me—and this is great news for all of us. Anyone can write a story. Anyone can write a pretty good story and many, many authors do. What they can't write is *your* good story. Only you have the qualifications to write that.

REAL WORLD EXAMPLES

Here are two examples of how adding my personal quirks made better stories:

Case Study 1: I was asked to write a Christmas story for children. I'm not a fan of the frenetic hustle of Christmas so I imagined what my happy holiday would look like. I would be alone on a mountain with no electricity. In fact, a year of that sounded nice—and there would be spiders because I like them better than Christmas. *The Christmas Spiders,* a revamp of an old Eastern European folktale, is now my secret, best selling book every holiday season.

Case Study 2: I took an older story I had about a male janitor with a chance for revenge and rewrote it adding in my personal experiences. I was once a janitor so I changed the protagonist to a middle aged woman suffering from an insufferable, sexist boss… just like my real life boss at that time. The entire story changed and became much better. It's now called "Just Us League" and it's published in *Giving the Devil His Due*. Anyone can tell the story of a janitor with a chance for revenge. Only I could tell "Just Us League."

YOUR TAKEAWAY TASK

Make a list of things you love and then take a look at your body of work. Can you see where you can add in your personal authenticity to create a story only you can tell? Don't just relate details of your life unless you're writing a memoir. Just lend personal elements of yourself to your worlds and characters. What parts of your personal experience could add depth to your work?

Here's your assignment. Take any common trope and add one of your hobbies. A vampire that loves knitting? A werewolf that rescues dogs? A zombie who enjoys cooking? I would read any of these. The real, authentic you makes everything better.

4

Who Wants to Be Read Forever?

W riting with significance creates writers of significance. Just as important as why you write is why you want to write any particular story at any particular time. The reason seems straightforward—a magazine is having open submissions and you want to to be published in it so you can add it to your bio. Maybe the pay is decent or you simply want the exposure. Those are good reasons, but there are some even better ones.

The act of creativity is transformative for both the creator and the recipient. When we write, we are pulling our thoughts to the page to share. Anyone who reads our work, for better or worse, is changed somehow. As Carl Jung famously said, "The meeting of two personalities is like the contact of two chemical substances: if there is any reaction, both are transformed." We are at our best when the transformations we inspire are positive.

POSITIVE CHANGE IS NOT LIMITED BY GENRE

Positive change does not mean warm and fuzzy. Change is messy and painful because it's growth. Horror writers might feel they can't have a positive impact because the genre revolves around terrible topics. This is confusing "warm and fuzzy" with positive.

A recent study shared from the National Center for Biotechnology

Information (NCBI) determined that fans of horror, particularly the morbidly curious, exhibited much higher resilience during the pandemic. In their own words: "We also found that morbid curiosity, a personality trait that has been previously associated with interest in horror (Scrivener, in press), was associated with greater positive resilience during the COVID-19 pandemic." (full study here) What's positive about horror? It shows how to face fear and defeat it and this is vital information even if it's not pleasant. Warm and fuzzy things get eaten. Positive change empowers.

Romance is another genre that gets overlooked as a vehicle for meaningful change. I'm guilty of discounting the power of romance. It was an elderly woman in the beginning of the 2020 pandemic lock down that changed my perspective. She came into the library to return a huge stack of pulpy romance novels. I'm sure I looked smug, given the dismissive thoughts going through my mind. "I'm sure I wouldn't know what to do if I didn't have these books to keep me occupied," she told me. "I'd probably do myself in." Well played, small elderly woman. She shocked and horrified a horror writer.

According to Digital History, "Hollywood played a valuable psychological role during the Great Depression. It provided reassurance to a demoralized nation. Even at the deepest depths of the Depression, 60 to 80 million Americans attended movies each week." (Digital History) If keeping hope and morale alive weren't enough, the romance genre is well known for addressing social issues such as race and class disparity from the beginning.

To me it's good news that we don't have to choose between writing what we feel called to and writing work that calls others. Genre fiction especially holds the power to empower simply because it's universally accepted and enjoyed by a mass audience.

CHANGE THE STORY, CHANGE THE WORLD

I like how Terry Pratchett puts it in *A Hat Full of Sky*... "The sun coming up every day is a story. Everything's got a story in it. Change the story, change the world." I think every writer seeks to produce their best. We invest in editing, proofreaders, cover designers, formatters... whatever it takes to show off our finest work. But what if that work had a chance to open minds, expand viewpoints and expose devolved idealism? Folding this power into your story brings it to the next level and can make it timeless.

Not every story has to change the world, but the ones that do last generations. Make your work matter and remain relevant. If you could say something to change the world, what would that be? Now add that message into your work. Think back to the stories that have stayed with you. More than likely they changed you somehow and that's why they stick. We entertain, but we can also teach, open minds and inspire. Our readers will return the love by remembering us long after that final page turns. Writing to change the world can help your stories have a permanent place in it.

YOUR TAKEAWAY TASK

Think of all the things you wish you could change. Injustices, ignorance, poverty, racism, animal cruelty… these are all powerful touch points. Look at how they could be woven into any story to expand on that message. This doesn't need to be a soap box rant. As Mary Poppins would say, a spoonful of sugar is needed.You are slipping your message into a bigger package. I've included a list of books that blend story and social message well at the end of this post.

As an exercise, try playing with social justice ideas and tropes you are familiar with. How could a little awareness of environmental destruction accent a vampire story? They've been around awhile and would notice the effects of climate change. How might a werewolf react if he came to demolish a village suffering from food insecurity or clean water? Personally, I'd love to hear Frankenstein comment on healthcare.

You don't have to use your stories as sleeper agents for positive change but fiction that impacts a reader on this level gets remembered for generations. Here's a list of books that have done just that and left the world a better place for being written:

1. *1984* by George Orwell
2. *Uncle Tom's Cabin* by Harriet Beecher Stowe
3. *To Kill a Mocking Bird* by Harper Lee
4. *The Grapes of Wrath* by John Steinbeck
5. *Things Fall Apart* by Chinua Achebe
6. *The Jungle* by Upton Sinclair
7. *The House of God* by Samuel Shem
8. *The Fire in the Flint* by Walter White
9. *Crime and Punishment* by Fyodor Dostoyevsky
10. *Lady Chatterley's Lover* by D.H. Lawrence

5

The What & Who: Genre & Reader

T his is one of those topics that suffers from the Popular Girl Paradox—
no one asks her to the party because everyone assumes she's been
asked to the party. I see a lot of questions concerning reader
preferences, genre and what defines genre which reminds me it wasn't that
long ago I was asking these questions myself.

The first time someone referred to me as a "speculative author" I had to go
look the term up, and even then I had questions. Did they mean I wasn't a real
writer because I was speculative, or did that mean I was a risky investment?
That led me down the rabbit hole of genre and I think at one point my
"genre" had turned into something like "paranormal conflict relationship
with supernatural and vampiric involvement." Wait… was this a genre or a
terrible blurb?

It's as important to understand the *what* we write—the genre—as it is to
understand the *why* we covered in WHY DO WE WRITE? Equally important
is the *who* are we writing for—the reader. It all seems pretty simple once
understood, but until then we spend a lot of time pushing the wrong pages
under the wrong noses.

An important thing to know and remember about genre is excellent writing
doesn't over rule reader preference. A personal example: I don't care for
romance. I've been married twice but I've never owned a wedding dress. I'm
happily married but we don't do anything for Valentine's Day. I'm happy.

In my reading, I want to explore what I don't know. What is the monster, how does it operate, what motivates it? This has me turning pages. Will this couple hook up and find true love? Sorry, did you say something? My attention was elsewhere.

Because of this, the best written romance book in the world will probably not lure me in. Trying to convince me to read a romance novel is like telling a vegan they will enjoy meat if they can just be open to the experience. You know that old joke about the guy trying to convince a lesbian she just hasn't had the right man? Trying to foist your book on someone who doesn't read your genre is *almost* as cringe worthy.

We are who we are and, after our adolescent years, we know what we want. It's not a judgment on a genre when someone doesn't prefer it. It's not a judgment on you as a writer when someone doesn't appreciate your genre. It's not personal, it's a personal preference.

Step one to planning your story, before you start in your outline, is to know *what* you're writing, the genre, and for who, the reader. If you are writing something in the romance genre, you might lose your reader when your protagonist turns out to have the rotting corpse of her ex lover in the basement... but if you are writing horror you will lose your reader by *not* having that well spoiled relationship hidden in the crawl space.

In conjunction with knowing your genre, it's just as important to know your reader. I found this out the hard way when I worked as a librarian. A teenager asked me for a horror book, something that would really terrify him—his own words. I gave him Clive Barker. He never talked to me again, turned the book in half read and mentioned to a few of the other librarians I shouldn't be making book recommendations. I could argue that he asked for something to terrify him, but that can mean something very different to a preschooler, adult or high schooler. I should have asked more questions and really gotten to know the reader before I just gave him a nightmare inducing book.

When you start trying to define genre, it can get tricky. I've seen people claim there are anywhere from 5 to 14 main genre categories with a plethora of subcategories and they tend to go all over. Here's a pretty common organizational list of *some* the main genres:

- Fiction
- Speculative—Horror, Science Fiction, Fantasy
- Literary
- Romance/Chick Lit
- Western
- Historical
- Mystery
- Thriller
- Nonfiction
- Biography/Autobiography/Memoir
- Review
- Teaching/How To
- Philosophy/Religion
- Self Help
- Journal
- Guide
- Poetry
- Speculative—Horror, Science Fiction, Fantasy
- Epic
- Satirical
- Political/Revolutionary
- Narrative
- Prose
- Lyrical

YOUR TAKEAWAY TASK

Think about the story you want to write and define the genre as closely as you can. If you think you are writing a horror book but there is a prominent relationship aspect, you might be creating a paranormal romance. Horror fans will be disappointed, and paranormal fans won't pick up your book because it looks horror. Be honest with yourself and your work. No genre is better than the other, so there is no reason to force yourself in one or the other.

After you have your genre nailed down and have familiarized yourself with the parameters, think of the reader you are writing for. There is a helpful practice in marketing where a product team will make up a hypothetical customer. They list the attributes, education levels and even come up with a name to encapsulate who that individual represents. It's not a bad idea to do that for your readers until you establish your audience in your mind. If you are writing for young horror readers, you might gloss over some of the gore. If you are writing for older horror readers, the gore will be your gloss.

6

On Jacket Copy & Elevator Pitches

You might be wondering why you would write jacket copy and your elevator pitch when your story isn't written yet? This is valid. It may seem early in the game, but doing this helps you be ahead of the game from the start. The jacket copy is more than a mini-plot on the back of your dust jacket. It's also a handy but often overlooked developmental tool. When written first, this small block of text can show you where your story falls flat. It's also just nice to have it done. I find it harder to do after the story is done because, by then, I'm over it.

Having the jacket copy written helps you define the focus of your story. It helps you see where your story may have plot holes or overused tropes. When you have to distill your entire story arc into a few paragraphs, there's an extra layer of focus during the creativity process to help an author stay on track. Just remember, once written, nothing is set in stone. Feel free to tweak, add and delete parts of the story that aren't working. As a side benefit, this also sets you up for success in case you get an opportunity to talk to an agent or editor about your book—and that can happen when you least expect it.

This is another good reason to have your elevator pitch nailed down early. Every reader and potential reader is important, and during the writing process there are plenty of opportunities to convert casual conversations into future fans... if you are prepared.

When I first started my career as a fiction author, I was unprepared. Someone would ask me what I do and I would mention that I write, usually while trying to shrink into my clothes and be invisible. If I could vanish I'd have extra time to think of words as my inner impostor screamed at me. If the someone persisted and asked me what I wrote I always had a terrible answer:

Potential reader: Oh, you are a writer? How exciting! What do you write?

Me: Oh, just some story about a girl who ran into the devil, but she didn't really have any faith so I kind of just wanted to see what happens. You know, it's fun. It passes the time.

Awkward pause

Me: I'm just playing with fiction. It's not very good. There are worse things I can be doing, right? I'll give you a free copy if you want…

Said person walks away as they make a mental note to never mention writing to me again.

By the time I was working on *Bitter Suites* I was better prepared. Someone would ask me what I was working on and I would answer this, my practiced elevator pitch:

This novella takes place in a hotel that specializes in recreational suicide, but not in a negative way. The question I wanted to answer was what if advanced technology could give us the ability to make it a return trip after death? Maybe we could get the urge to self-harm out of our system. If we could prove to ourselves how devastating the act is and how it changes nothing, I'd hope we could move forward to a healthier place. So that's why I'm writing this book. The Bitter Suites is the hotel where I hope people can explore their self destructive impulses in a safe place—fiction.

I never had a person walk away from that elevator pitch. That novella went on to be the only self-published novel on the Bram Stoker Awards® Finalist ballot and had an incredible agent and two well established, award winning publishers interested in the second book in the series, *Suite & Sour*.

Feel free to ask me to ask me anytime why I didn't land that awesome agent and publishing deal. That needs to be a chapter all on its own in a different book, but the short answer is I became convinced I would die in the pandemic and panic-published towards the end of 2020. Lesson learned. That went on my list of things not to do..

But back to being prepared and polished. I hope I've made a good case for why you should write your jacket copy and elevator pitch before you write your book. Even if you are just doing a short story, an elevator pitch is good to have ready. Potential readers are everywhere. They can be disguised as neighbors, cashiers or the person next to you on the bus. Get other people excited about your story and you will have a line of readers waiting.

Ultimately you, as the author, are the product you are trying to promote. As the Golden Goose, you have many stories to tell in a lifetime. Don't turn off future readers by stuttering lukewarm nonsense when they ask what your story is about. I've been there, done that and I don't recommend it.

Now that you know why to write jacket copy and an elevator pitch before you write your story, here's how. For such short pieces of wordage, we writers have all sorts of anxiety when creating them. There are thousands of blog posts, videos, essays and forums to tell you the nuts and bolts of creating these, but they primarily say the same thing.

Jacket Copy: No more than 200 words, max. This is the text that goes on the back of your book and most likely will be used as the book description online. It should cover the exciting points of your story without giving away spoilers. Short, the entire point of this small block of text is to excite, so don't bother describing a heroine's brilliant blue eyes and lustrous locks unless they have something to do with the story. You will often see jacket copy end with a cliffhanger question. There's a reason for that. It's a call to action that directs the reader to explore more. Will our heroine make it through the zombie apocalypse to find undead true love on the other side? Invite the reader to find out.

Elevator Pitch: Short and concise is key here. The elevator pitch got its name from being about the length of an elevator ride with a captive agent or editor. Narrow your pitch down to the things that strike a nerve. This is bait on the end of a hook. The fish doesn't ask the worm for a resume. It just wants to know if he's tasty. Same thing with your pitch. This is the hook you drop when someone asks you in the coffee line what you are working on. This is more than just reciting what your story is about. In that case, my *Bitter Suites* pitch would have been:

My story is about a recreational suicide hotel run by a woman named Azrael. Her guests can choose what kind of death they want from a variety of package deals. While the hotel guests change from chapter to chapter, there is a central, unnamed character that continues on in a connected narrative that demonstrates how addictive behavior can destroy self esteem and ruin our lives. The purpose of the story is to allow people entertaining the idea of self harm to safely role play what the real consequences are in hopes it may prompt them to reconsider. This is a story meant to take the glamour away from death.

That's what the story is about, essentially, but I don't think the guy in line with me will be caught by that. He needs to know the mic drop details: recreational suicide. Those two things don't go together. The two contrast, negative and positive. Curiosity engaged. Potential reader hooked.

While there is a certain amount of value in shock, use it sparingly. Don't come in so edgy you have your listener backing away and looking for the nearest exit. This is why I would quickly add "but not in a negative way." The listener is engaged because they want to find out what could possibly be positive about something so horrible. So I tell them, only with fictional technology is this currently possible and I emphasize (because it is a dangerous topic) that the hope with this story is that it will be a therapeutic exploration, not a glorification.

It's important to be honest in your pitch as well. If someone is looking for a book that romanticizes self harm, they won't like the book I wrote. It also doesn't hurt to add any positive mentions you've gotten from other authors. Please never say your friends or mother liked it, even if they do.

YOUR TAKEAWAY TASK

Write the jacket copy and share with anyone that will read it and note their reactions. Were they interested, confused or bored? You don't want that friend that will tell you this is the best sounding book they've ever heard of. You want someone that will give you honest, constructive feedback. If you receive comments suggesting they've already heard stories like this, you might need to tweak your ideas to be more original and engaging. This is easy right now, before you've written a word. The jacket copy is like the address of your story. It informs the reader where this story lives, and in what part of town. It invites them to visit.

With your elevator pitch, practice this until you can say it naturally and out of order if needed. It should sound spontaneous, like you just thought of it. The idea isn't to repeat the 30 seconds verbatim. It's to generate interest. Make it a game with your friends to repeat your pitch often and in answer to unrelated questions. Say it in the mirror, record yourself and then start practicing on strangers any chance you get. It's better to freeze up with the lady next to you on the bus than a potential publisher. If the jacket copy is the address, the elevator pitch is the key that unlocks the door for the reader. Not only do you need to have it ready, you need to know how to make it click.

7

Hurting Heroes, Happy Readers

"Stories about contented people are miserably dull," says Orson Scott Card. In other words, the character who suffers the most will catch the most attention. People who suffer don't want things to stay the same—they want change. Readers pick up books to read about change. Without it, what's the point? Your protagonist will be as interesting as a pet rock.

Poor Frodo suffered the most of any of the Fellowship. Not only did he endure physical pain like cold, hunger and giant Shelob bites but he suffered emotionally as well. He was a reluctant adventurer. He didn't want to leave the Shire, but if he hadn't there would be no story.

HARDWIRED FOR RUBBERNECKING

Lisa Cron talks about this in her excellent book, *Wired for Story*. Backed by neuroscience, Cron breaks down the elements of story that keep a reader glued to the page, and a major hook is a protagonist's pain. "It lets us sit back and vicariously experience someone else suffering the slings and arrows of outrageous fortune, the better to learn how to dodge those darts should they ever be aimed at us," she says.

The brain uses story as role play. More than entertainment, a story is tasked with creating *what if* scenarios, and the more difficult the better. Watching a heroine defeat a dragon gives clues on how to defeat a bully. If Frodo can take on Mount Doom, then surely Monday is survivable. Growing up, stories are passed on to us as cautionary tales. Don't stray too far—there are monsters in the forest.

As a writer it can be tempting to pull our punches with our own protagonists. Often they are a facet of us, their creator. We know Frodo has to get to Mount Doom but did the orcs have to steal his clothes? Few things are worse than being on an arduous quest... nude. According to Lisa Cron, "A story is an escalating dare, and its goal is to make sure your protagonist is worthy of her goal."

KICK THEM WHEN THEY'RE DOWN

In Stephen King's Carrie, the titular character has the odds stacked miles high against her: religious zealot for a mother, poor, adolescent, homely, awkward. Just when you think it can't get any worse for this poor kid, she has her first period in a public high school shower. But wait, there's more. Because her mother is a zealot, she hasn't been educated about this feminine coming of age moment so she panics and begs her classmates for help only to be bombed with sanitary pads and derision.

Whether or not a reader has ever experienced menstruation, we all feel the pain of humiliation, terror and being unloved. It's the vulnerability and suffering of Carrie that draws us to the story. We empathize, we care and we want her to find justice. If King had let up on the poor girl, her story wouldn't be remembered now, nearly five decades later.

Pain doesn't have to be physical to be effective. When I read about poor Frodo stripped naked in front of his captors, as a body-shy teenage girl I cringed. To me, that was the worst thing imaginable. You could have burned me alive but I would bet money my adolescent defiance would have won. Make me stand naked before my enemies, however, and I would've spilled the location of my secret base in exchange for a baggy sweater. Tolkien was relentless in ratcheting up the pain for Frodo, even to the last scene. Because of this, generations all over the world are still reading about Hobbits..

LAYER THE PAIN

When your characters figure their way out of one terrible situation, make it a doorway into the next. Take their suffering, salt it and then slap on another layer. Readers will devour the results. A good example of this is *The Natural* by Bernard Malamud. The story centers around a gifted baseball player named Roy Hobbs. His worst fear is realized when he loses his spot in the big leagues through no fault of his own. Physically attacked, he loses his ability to play the game he loves, and the only thing he's really good at. But wait, there's more!

Malamud knew that was a surface level tragedy. To really keep the reader hooked, he layered the suffering. Later in life the down-and-out ball player has a chance to play again but it's tainted when he's offered a huge amount of money to throw the game. Guilt, shame, derision, disappointment…Hobbs suffers. At the last moment he has a redemptive moment. Perhaps a happy ending? Nope. His attempt at redemption fails as well and he walks away a completely broken man. No career, no possibility to regain his honor and one last, fat failure… and readers have been turning those pages since 1952.

Think about this whenever your own characters face discomfort. How can you ratchet it up? If your hero has been stabbed, twist their ankle as they evade. If they are hungry, let them find a box of cookies that turns out to be empty when they open it. Better, let it be their favorite cookie that brings back memories of the *one* time they were happy. The empty box is a soul crushing moment. Knock them down so low they can't possibly go on… but they do.

That's what makes them a hero… and worth reading repeatedly.

YOUR TAKEAWAY TASK

Next week we will be ready to outline a story using all the things we've learned up to now. Start thinking of the type of story you would like to write and how it affects your career (WHY WRITE?). If your goal is to make money, research what's trending right now to boost your product marketability. If it's to inspire or teach, consider how you can add that content into this project.

Then consider what parts of you would make this story unique? There's nothing new under the sun, but only you can tell your story (YOU ARE THE SECRET PLOT TWIST). Finally, decide if there is a way to weave significance into your story. Is there a message you'd like to pass on to the world to make it better? How about a warning, a judgment? When you shine a light on what you think should be seen, sometimes it can shine a lasting light on your work (WHO WANTS TO BE READ FOREVER?)

8

Outline 101: Pantsers & Plotters

Which is better, pantsers or plotters?

There's arguments for both sides. Among famous and successful plotters we have John Grisham and R.L. Stein. On the pantser side we have the likes of Stephen King and Margaret Atwood. Both sides have prominent champions and valid arguments

But this is me assuming that you are familiar with the writer terms *pantser* and *plotter*. If not, you aren't alone. The first time I heard them I hit up Google. Simply put, a plotter is someone that makes a detailed outline of their book before they write it. A pantser just runs with it by the seat of their pants, allowing their muse to guide them. So now that we are clear on what they are, let's hear some arguments for both.

PANTSER VS PLOTTER

Representing Team Pro-Plotter

"The more time I spend on the outline the easier the book is to write. And if I cheat on the outline I get in trouble with the book." —John Grisham

"If you do enough planning before you start to write, there's no way you can have writer's block. I do a complete chapter by chapter outline." —R.L. Stein

You can't argue with that logic, can you? And both writers have the track record to back them. But what about the other side of the coin?

Speaking for Team Pro-pantser

[A story begins with] "an image, scene, or voice…I couldn't write the other way round with structure first. It would be too much like paint-by-numbers." —Margaret Atwood

"Outlines are the last resource of bad fiction writers who wish to God they were writing masters' theses." —Stephen King

Also good points. So which is better? Pantsing or plotting? The answer is… it depends. Whatever works for you on your current project. And yes, that does sound like a cop-out.

The bottom line is writing is hard, and whatever gets the right words to the page is what you should do. Something important to realize is that nothing about writing (or creating in general) is static. What worked for you today may not work tomorrow. What worked for a short story may not work for a novel.

The best answer I have is to allow yourself to be flexible. Don't beat yourself up because you didn't make an outline if it's working for you. And if you start deviating from your outline, that's okay too as long as it's working. I can't tell you *what* to do because I'm not you. I can only tell you what works for me. I've been both pantser and plotter and I tend to produce my best work with a hybrid approach of the two.

FANCY PANTSING & PLOTTY HUMOR

My first book (*End of Mae*) was pure pantsing. I decided to write a fiction book and it began with me wondering what would happen if someone who didn't believe in Satan actually met Satan? And with that, I started writing. It took me many years to write that novella. Halfway through I realized one of my subplots was boring so I chopped out a complete story line. Three quarters of the way through I realized I had no idea what the point was anymore, and by the time I got to the end I was relieved.

The benefit was letting the characters have their own life. They constantly surprised me with their decisions during the creation. On the other hand, I wasted a lot of time writing useless sections only to delete them later. I could never make a living as a pure pantser because it just wasn't efficient for me.

Flash forward to *Suite & Sour*, the follow up to *Bitter Suites*. I had a glorious outline. I wrote the book in two weeks. I also didn't enjoy it as much. As Atwood put it, it did feel like painting-by-numbers. I was a director of someone's story. *"In this scene, Azrael needs to discover the betrayal and shatter a bottle of absinthe so we can justify using the pun as the chapter title. Okay... action"* It turned out fine, but the process wasn't as enjoyable for me. If I don't have fun then it means I'm actually working for a living. I've tried that and I don't like it.

PLANNING PANTSERS—PLANTSERS?

Flash forward to now. What works well for me currently is a hybrid of pantser and plotter. Maybe I need to coin a new term: plantser? A planning pantser? This is what I use currently and I'm turning out my best work efficiently and with much joy. As a note, this is how I approach longer fiction. For nonfiction, I have a much stricter outline. For short fiction I have more of a Post-It note scribble thing.

So for longer fiction, the focus of this chapter:

First I think of my general idea. I might need a story about a fictional war that makes a statement on current issues but without clubbing the reader to death with a soapbox. I start jotting ideas. Who is my protagonist? What do they need? Where is their pain? Where do I start with that pain? And then I start jotting down where the story starts. It's full of misspellings, half-baked concepts and is a grammatical nightmare. After I get that first start down, I ask the magic question: *and then?*

This leads me down a chain of cause and effect. I don't worry if it sounds cliche, trite, unbelievable… that will all be polished out in the final step which I'll be covering next week. At this point, what I've written down sounds like a half dozen stories I could name. Then I go back to the start and I rework it a second time. I make sure that if in my third chapter she needs a boat, then she needs to procure a boat in chapter one or two. I read this over a few times and looking at it from above I can see where a baby brother may need to be added in. Because I'm outlining, I can easily pop that baby brother in, or delete him. This is a lot easier than deleting 20k words when you realize the homeless woman's subplot just isn't working.

At this point, it's still very rough, and very loose. Actually, who am I kidding? It will remain rough and loose. For me, it's more of a guideline than an outline. I know the events I need to have so this story can progress in a somewhat linear fashion from Point A to Point B. As I write, I often deviate. I know my protagonist needs to make a friend that dies in the next chapter so the guilt can factor into her actions. In my guide/outline, that individual is attacked by a beast. As I actually write, that character is caught in the friendly fire. The result is the same, the journey isn't.

I'm not trapped in my outline, but because I know where I'm going, I can get there fast, somewhat stress free and effectively. But this is not the end of outlining. The second half of the outlining process I cover next week is where the scientifically proven magic goes in. Since I started going over my guide/outlines a third time with a different purpose, my story quality has shot way up. And when I say I'm going over this outline three times, it's usually pretty quick. A half hour tops, just to get the guts pinned down so I know where to start adding flesh.

YOUR TAKEAWAY TASK

It's finally time to put pen to paper and fingers to the keyboard. This week, think of your story and the best approach for it—pantsing or plotting. While you may decide this process isn't for you, try a rough guide/outline to help you define your direction. It's not meant to be a brilliant best seller at this point. Just put down who you want to get where and do what when. Make sure you add plenty of typos to remind yourself that you're human.

9

Advanced Outlines: Layering for Depth

So now you have a basic story outline. A protagonist gets from Point A to Point B and some things happen in between. At this point, I suggest you pick up a copy of *Wired for Story* by Lisa Cron. Her book reveals the cognitive secrets of what hooks us into any given story. I'm going to cover some of the basics that I've built into my personal methodology but Lisa Cron's book is a brilliant study of how the human brain works and how it reacts to elements of story—and why.

But right now, a demonstration of how layering around your basic outline creates depth without pulling your hair out. I'm going to use a minimal outline as an example: Poor Boy meets Rich Girl. Poor Boy must defeat insurmountable odds to date Rich Girl. Poor Boy changes his fate and dates Rich Girl..

1. **Poor Boy meets Rich Girl.**
2. **Poor Boy must defeat insurmountable odds to win Rich Girl.**
3. **Poor Boy changes his fate and dates Rich Girl.**

This is a very basic plot that's been played out a million times. Because it's so basic, it's easy to customize. Writers take this simple plot and add layers and depth to it. If they do that well, the story line stands alone, individual and intoxicating. Examples of stories like this are *A Knight's Tale*, *The Princess Bride*, *Dirty Dancing*, *Grease* and *Aladdin*.

I used movies so you can quickly go watch these to break out the different story elements that keep you hooked. Would you say any of these movies are like each other other than being about a poor boy falling in love above his station? I wouldn't.

STICK THE PROTAGONIST, HOOK THE READER

Now to add the layering. To hook readers, every story must elicit emotion, follow cause and effect, and have difficult trials to overcome. The reader must be able to have empathy with the protagonist so they care about the consequences. Bad things must happen to your protagonist repeatedly. Let them get out of their frying pans by jumping into their fires. And then have hot oil splat on them followed by the cat catching them, a good mauling and then the ultimate indignity of being spat out, half-digested in a hairball.

That's all external conflict, but a story must elicit emotion as well. If the reader isn't caring, they aren't sharing in the experience and will lose interest. A good way to get emotional attachment is with internal conflict. If a man jumps out of a moving car to escape a serial killer it's interesting. If a man jumps out of a moving car to escape a serial killer *in spite of* his clinical road rash phobia, the reader forms an emotional bond. I mean, it's logical. Who isn't a little afraid of road rash?

Going back to the protagonist in the pan, if they have a phobia of fire, it would be almost impossible to get them to jump out of that pan. Imagine the agony of fear and sizzling feet. When they finally do jump, they make it just past the flames… only to be splashed in the hot oil. The reason they had a phobia of fires was because their poor mother was disfigured by a terrible cooking oil accident and your protagonist grew up affected by Mother's shame of her appearance.

We covered how important it is to hurt your protagonists physically and emotionally in HURTING HEROES, HAPPY READERS. That post tells you *why* you should hurt your heroes. Now we learn *how* to hurt our heroes.

The point of this is to show how adding a little internal conflict (phobia of fire, childhood trauma) makes for a richer and more engaging plot. Back to our Poor Boy story. Let's layer in some of the elements we just talked about.

1. **Poor Boy meets Rich Girl.**
2. Shame at his lack of means prompts him to fake his wealth.
3. **Poor Boy must defeat insurmountable odds to win Rich Girl.**
4. Needing money to afford the date, Poor Boy keeps a wallet he finds in the bathroom, despite being an honest guy.
5. **Poor Boy changes his fate and dates Rich Girl.**
6. Poor Boy takes Rich Girl on a nice date.

Better, but now let's add in some *more* pain and conflict.

1. **Poor Boy meets Rich Girl.**
2. Shame at his lack of means prompts him to fake his wealth.
3. His gross bravado makes Rich Girl think he's a jerk. She agrees to go out with him with the intention of humiliating him.
4. **Poor Boy must defeat insurmountable odds to win Rich Girl.**
5. Needing money to afford the date, Poor Boy keeps a wallet he finds in the bathroom despite being an honest guy.
6. As he's flashing his ill gotten cash he runs into his poor friend, a waiter, who asked for a loan earlier but Poor Boy said he had nothing to give him.
7. **Poor Boy changes his fate and dates Rich Girl.**
8. Poor Boy takes Rich Girl on a nice date.
9. Date is tainted when the angry friend/waiter points out what a jerk and a liar Rich Boy is to his date.

You can see where this is going, and it's nowhere good for Poor Boy until he winds up as a hero, performing an ultimate act of selflessness in the face of abject loss... and the tables get turned. I can see all sorts of room for more conflict and inner turmoil. What if Poor Boy had just written an essay on honesty to try for a scholarship? To appease the angry waiter friend, he tries to give him some cash but Rich Girl recognizes her dad's wallet. Poor Boy goes to jail. When the dad comes to pick up his wallet and confront the thief (who could have been a hero had he chosen the honest path) Poor Boy realizes the man is on the scholarship committee. All is lost: no girl, no friend, no scholarship. Every time he jumps out of the pan, the flames get hotter.

Layering in the conflicts around a basic story makes for an effective, engaging plot that gives a reader an emotional bond with the protagonist and keeps them turning pages. It makes it easy to see where emotional conflict can be added in, where the story might be sagging and keep track of subplots.

YOUR TAKEAWAY TASK

Watch one of the movies I named earlier and see if you can pick out the layers of internal and external conflict, the cause and effect logic and how many times the protagonist jumps out of the pan only to get burned worse. Then go over the basic outline you created last week and start adding in those layers. If your protagonist needs to get in a boat to escape something, create a solid reason they can't do it without internal struggle—leaving loved ones behind, fear of water, a monster is hunting, distrust of shipmates, leaky boat, premonition of doom... the possibilities are as wide as your imagination. Then rinse and repeat.

10

Never Shun the Shunn

Welcome to the best kept secret all the editors want you to know: formatting. Simply knowing how to format your work dramatically increases your story's chance of making it out of the slush pile and onto the shelf. Don't take my word for it. Ask any editor or publisher—a main reason stories get rejected is because they are improperly formatted.

A well formatted story uses Shunn, unless the editor specifies otherwise. The good news is not only is Shunn formatting free, but you can save a formatted template in your word processing program and always have submission ready work as soon as you hit THE END (after you go back to spell check and edit, of course). First, find a free Shunn formatting template online here: shunn.net/format/classic.

When I was first scolded for submitting an improperly formatted manuscript, I thought the editor was being an anal retentive jerk on a power trip. *Who cares about this formatting stuff,* I thought. *Words is words, man. If you can read it it should be good enough.*

A few years later when I became a fiction editor myself I learned just how important proper formatting is. To illustrate, let me tell you a small horror story to highlight the importance of why you must never shun the Shunn.

HOW I BECAME AN ANAL RETENTIVE EDITOR

I was in the final selection stage for *Space & Time* magazine and we had just started using a submissions grinder (Duotrope). Because I was unfamiliar with the system, I didn't realize I could ask for emails to be included with submissions. I also didn't realize I had no way of contacting the submitter after I hit accept or deny. And I was tired. The First Readers and Gerard Hourner, our Fictions Editor, had already done most of the work, combing through somewhere around 200 short stories. I only had about 20 to read, but I was still tired.

I found one I really liked—we will call the author Bob Smith—and sent him the automatic acceptance letter. This is where it gets horrible. I hadn't paid attention to his formatting. My thoughts at the time were if I can read it, good enough for me to consider. I wasn't going to be one of those stick-in-the-mud editors. *Spoiler: I am now.* I copied up the acceptance email with a list of what I needed and realized... I didn't know where to send his email. He had no contact information on his document. Duotrope didn't have a way for me to contact him either, at least not that I could figure out.

No worries, I thought. *I'll look on Facebook.* This probably would have worked, except that he was a very new author and there were a lot of Bob Smiths. I started sending messages. I tried all the socials and found a lot of Bob Smiths, but none were the one I was looking for. In the meantime, I was making friends. One Bob Smith tried to sell me a gym membership in Australia. Another tried to sell me insurance. There were quite a few that were also authors, but not the one I was looking for. I answered questions about our magazine and writing in general but didn't find the right Bob Smith. If I hadn't already sent him an automatic acceptance letter, I would have tossed his story in the bin and selected someone else even though I liked it.

I think it took me about two weeks to find the right author. In the process I spent a lot of time and stress searching. This was time I needed to spend on other magazine duties and my own writing. The ending turned out fine and Bob Smith and I both learned some valuable things. He received a lecture on Shunn formatting and I learned *why* it was so important.

THE MORE YOU KNOW

"No one knows how many good stories are passed over because the manuscripts containing them are poorly formatted," writes William Shunn. "We can be certain, however, that editors will more eagerly read a cleanly formatted manuscript than a cluttered and clumsy one."

Thousands of manuscripts are rejected everyday because they lack formatting, but it's one of the easiest and best things to do to boost your chances. Sadly, many of the rejected stories are probably excellent and worthy of publishing—they just lacked the formatting. At the end of this post I have an example screenshot of what I use myself with my actual contact information, which is public. You are absolutely invited to send me an email or a snail mail letter to let me know what you think of this book, if it's helped you at all or ask questions.

If I were asked what is the number one, best way an author can boost their chances of getting published my answer would be to properly format your work. An experienced editor can see at a glance who is new, and possibly going to be a lot of extra work. On the other hand, a well formatted document is a joy and an editor will pull it out of the slush on that merit alone and give it a closer read.

A HAPPY EDIT ENDING STORY

I can't share the potential sad story of Bob Smith without sharing a positive example to support my soapbox platform. A few issues after the Bob Smith incident I got another submission from a Leonard Spieser. This was a properly formatted manuscript down to the Times New Roman 12 point font. I read it, loved it. Not only was the formatting done right but so was the story.

Plenty of interior and exterior conflict, believable dialogue and it was a highly innovative perspective that handled some delicate social justice issues without fanning any unnecessary flames. Then I found out this was Speiser's first fiction story. I was so impressed, I interviewed him as a success story and brought him on as a columnist. The story is well worth checking out: "interference" by Leonard Speiser in *Space & Time*, Issue #139–Winter 2020.

It's your choice whether you want to impress the editors or annoy them, but I strongly suggest you go for the first option. Editors are people. While they are reading your work they have dishes stacking up, kids yelling in the next room and their own deadlines. They are often doing this to help other writers, which they are probably doing it for free. The easier you can make things for them, the more they will appreciate you. As an author hoping to sell your story, that is a good place to be.

YOUR TAKEAWAY TASK

If you haven't already, go to shunn.net/format/classic. Open your word processing software and create a blank page. Copy and paste the Shunn example just past the first few lines and paste it in your blank document. Personalize it with your own information. Now save it with a name you will remember. Mine has "template" in the file name. Whenever I start a new story, the first thing I do is copy and paste my Shunn template text into a new document. I update the title if I know it and I start typing. Begin your own Shunn template now and don't be a Bob Smith.

11

Broken First Lines Make Good Hooks

In fiction, a first sentence should entangle the reader in lies without misleading.

Hopefully, my first sentence did exactly that—entangle you. If I did my job right, you want to know what I meant and where this is going. Your brain is pondering how being caught in a web of lies can be anything but misleading.

What sticks with your more… that perfect date or the beautiful disaster? Same thing with your story's first line—it's your pick up line for readers. Perfect is nice, but something broken we remember.

That first sentence can be the hardest of the whole book. There is a lot of pressure on those initial words. They have to set a tone for the entire story. They should be memorable. Most important, your opening has to hook the reader with honest intent. Let's break this down.

SETTING A TONE

From my first sentence, you could expect this post to be concise and to the point. I cut out a lot of words I could have used. Instead of using the tired out "web of lies," I implied this with the verb *entangled*. You might expect it to be informational, surprising and maybe even a little poetic. I could have easily just said *The first sentence of your story should hook your reader while setting the tone*, but I like to play with words and I hope you, as my reader, do as well.

My intent was to project that this is going to be a surprising, intelligent piece that will give you something to think about. Let's see if I can follow through.

STRIVE FOR IMPERFECTION

While my first line can't possibly compete with the greats like Tolkien, Dickens and Orwell, hopefully by next week you will still remember the gist of it if it came up in conversation. What makes a first line memorable? The best first lines have something that doesn't belong. It's human nature to seek perfection, but perfection dams us to mediocrity.

Think about these memorable first lines:

"I am an invisible man"
  Invisible Man by Ralph Ellison (1952)

"It was the best of times, it was the worst of times..."
  A Tale of Two Cities, Charles Dickens (1859)

'Mother died today. Or maybe, yesterday; I can't be sure'
  The Outsider by Albert Camus (1942)

'It was a bright cold day in April, and the clocks were striking thirteen'
  1984 by George Orwell (1949)

'I write this sitting in the kitchen sink'
  I Capture the Castle by Dodie Smith (1948)

"In a hole in the ground there lived a hobbit."
  The Hobbit, J.R.R. Tolkien (1937)

In each of these iconic first lines, something doesn't fit. A man can't be invisible, times can't be best and worst, you must know when your mother died, clocks don't strike thirteen… but it's exactly this inconsistency, the wrongness, that hooks the brain and holds it captive. As writers, that is our goal.

To create your own memorable first lines, just write the perfect line, and then break it. If your book starts with a thirsty character in a desert you could begin with *Bob is thirsty*. Or, *Bob was tired of drinking sand*. As a reader, the first line might remind me that I'm also thirsty and I put the book down. The second, broken line has me appalled. *What? People don't drink sand. What is this writer on about?* I continue reading. This is exactly what I did at the beginning of my 2018 novella, *Bitter Suites*:

"It was my 18th birthday, and I was finally going to die in a safe, monitored environment."

I don't have to break down all the things that don't belong in that sentence, but it worked. *Bitter Suites* was my first Bram Stoker Awards® Finalist.

LIE WITHOUT MISLEADING

If your story is fiction, you are lying. Fiction is make believe, fantasy, speculative… it's not real. It's all a lie built of many truths… but if you mislead your reader you will lose their trust and attention.

Even though a fiction writer is technically telling something not true, that first sentence still has to give the reader a promise of what's to come. How disappointing would it be to read George Orwell's creepy line about clocks striking thirteen, only to have it turn out to be a sweet romance? Close the book. What if Albert Camus caught your attention with his ambiguous statement of maternal death only to follow up with jokes? Close the book. Of Dickens following the best and worst of times with a happy story about a little girl that lives on the prairie? Close. The. Book.

That would be misleading, and your reader will not only close the book, but they might never pick up another one of yours.

YOUR TAKEAWAY TASK

Look up first lines that have stuck with you and see if they are somehow broken. Pick up random books and see how those lines sit with you. Would you remember this in a week? Would you tell a friend about it? How do the lines make you feel... like reading on or making a sandwich? Then write down some of your own lines and play.

12

Stick Your Ending, Stick Your Readers

As tricky as it is to begin a story, it's just as tricky to end it. Failure to stick your landing can lose your reader forever. They have gifted you with their time and attention. These are things they can't ever get back, and they chose to invest them with you. Don't pay them back with a shoddy ending. I speak from personal experience.

Years ago I wanted to have an excuse to be friends with another author I knew, so I read their book. I wanted it to be well done so I could gush over their work, and I wasn't disappointed. I loved everything about it and was caught up until the very last page... but it shouldn't have been the last page. The story wasn't over. Mid-action, no resolve, not even something ambiguous to ponder later—done. The lead protagonist was basically in mid-stride, fleeing for her life and then it was all over. I was so confused I thought my book was missing pages so I checked the table of contents. It was all there, but I no longer was. I was so disappointed I never read another book by that author, even after we did become friends.

How many other readers had the same reaction when they hit that unfinished ending? That author still struggles to get their books out there, and they have a lot of talent. They just can't stick their endings, and because of that, they can't stick their readers either.

Google *how to end a story* and you will find pages and pages of advice. How many ways are there to end a book? The list ranges anywhere from 4-6 ways.

Why is it so difficult to pin down an exact number? Because stories aren't manufactured, factory-style. I'm not going to claim I have a definitive list because I don't think there are a finite number of ways to end a book. They are crafted, every one. Even stories created by AI are unique and surprising.

For instance, what if you have a classic hero's journey story line. In the end, the hero has returned home, but so changed by his adventure he is no longer the same individual. Nice and resolved with all loose ends tied into a tidy bow. But you'd like to show the reader a glimpse into his future, so now it's resolved but also expanded with an epilogue. Maybe the reader is a little too comfortable, so you decide to give a whisper of threat in that ending. The villain has been defeated... or has he? Now it's unresolved.

If you haven't read the *Lord of the Rings* books, spoiler alert. At the end of J.R.R. Tolkien's *Return of the King*, Frodo and Sam are saved from the brink of death on the slopes of Mount Doom after a tearful farewell (unexpected). They are welcomed as heroes in Gondor and attend a grand wedding (resolved). Eventually they leave the party and take the meandering route home (not an epilogue, but expanded) only to find The Shire has been ruined by vengeful deeds. The hero hobbits once again save the day, but not for poor Frodo. Haunted by all the horror he has witnessed, he can't take part in the peace he has earned. Sad, but resolved... for a few years. Then Frodo hops ship with the elves to the Undying Lands to vanish on the horizon (ambiguous). So what kind of ending did Tolkien use? His own, a blend of many, and it works.

My point is, don't feel locked into an ending type. Listen to your story and let the ending (and the word count) be exactly what it needs to be. The story knows, and if you listen it will tell you. If you do feel stuck, here is a brief overview of some types of endings, but by all means not all. Your finale does depend on one thing, however: the end justifies the preceding events. It closes the story with relevance and adds meaning.

There are four primary ways to accomplish this:

The hero wins his goal (happy ending).

The hero loses his goal (unhappy ending).

The hero wins his goal but loses something of great value. (tragic ending)

The hero could win, but sacrifices his goal for a greater good. (inspirational ending)

These, and endless variations of these plot pillars become endings:

1. Resolved ending: no loose ends.
2. Unresolved ending: cliffhanger, good for series.
3. Expanded ending: as in an epilogue.
4. Unexpected ending: a surprise twist or reveal.
5. Ambiguous ending: open to interpretation.
6. Circular ending: ends where the story began.

Despite there being no finish to the infinite variations of potential endings, being familiar with the basics can help your story structure from the first page. Whether the story keeps winding on or feels abrupt, you can try on different finishes and see what feels right. There could be an issue at play in the plot you, as the writer, were unaware of.

Sometimes characters can shift in their ethical alignments without the writer being aware. Lawful good slides into chaotic good with just a few sarcastic remarks. That would be enough to invalidate a classic hero's journey finale and make it hard to close. However your story ends, ultimately it has to feel right to you. Certainly ask your beta readers how it sits with them, but remember whose story this is and stay true to it.

You are the magician that has created an incredible illusion. To let the ending flop is like promising doves and then pulling old feathers out of your sleeve. Unless you are a comedy act, you audience won't appreciate it, or be likely to return.

YOUR TAKEAWAY TASK

Grab some books off your shelf and read the endings with this list beside you. Try to pick out the different elements, or combination of, that lead a story to its finish. Then think of alternative endings and experiment with how that affects the entire piece. The ending may seem like nothing more than a last page to turn, but it's one of the most important parts of your story.

13

After The End

What do you do after you finally tap out those final words? The first and most important thing to realize is this is a first draft, and it needs some work. As you hold that ream of printed paper in your hands and reflect on all the hard work it took to produce, know that you have plenty more hard work ahead. But the hardest part is done and you are well on your way to fame and fortune, or at least some fun. Time to take a break.

REST, READ, & EVALUATE

Did the story stay true to the genre? If the answer is yes, you are golden. If the answer is no, you have some choices to make. When I wrote *Soft Deadlines* (available on Kindle Vella) I added in a gruesome nightmare scene that involved a giant silver praying mantis eating the heroine's head. The book is paranormal romance, so it shouldn't get too graphic. A demon incubus is fine, but no eating of brains. I had three choices: take it out, change the genre or leave it in and get angry reviews. I chose to take it out. If I had quite a few scenes like that, I probably would have swapped genre. I never want to mislead my readers. That's not fair to them.

As you read through your story, put on your editor's hat. Now it's time to get hard on yourself. Evaluate story line for passive voice, flat plot and opportunities to ramp up the pain. Do your protagonists change? Do they experience growth or do they devolve? It doesn't matter how they end up as long as they experience change. No one wants to read a story about a protagonist that remains unaffected by anything that transpires. Shake up their world and have them walk away differently. If they don't, you have some rewrites to do. Now is also when you want to go look at that cover copy and elevator pitch you wrote. How much has changed? Update it..

BETAS MAKE IT BETTER

Once you've done your polish, time to hit the pavement with it and recruit some beta readers. Here's where you get to practice that elevator speech. Hit up every bookworm you know. Query with elevator pitch. If they are interested, give them a copy with a deadline for when you need comments back. Many people use an easy and effective Google Docs system. Just send an email with a link to the chapter and then a link to the Google Form. Readers don't have to look for anything, just click, read, critique.

Once they start coming in, evaluate your beta reader's notes. Put the ego in a drawer and pay attention to their feedback. You are not obligated to use it all, and some you really may not agree with. Consider it all though. Discount nothing. If a reader didn't understand something, that's not because of their lack of comprehension. You need to explain it better. Make structural edits as needed.

Now, it's time for second edits. This will be your line edits. Line edits and structural edits are two completely different beasts and not all editors do both. When you are looking for a good editor, make sure you know what type of editing you seek. At this point, your manuscript should be polished enough to just be a matter of looking for typos, grammar and issues that spellcheck missed. Beg, borrow, barter or pay for a proofreader or two to make sure the end product is as clean as possible.

Notice how I don't use the word perfect? Even high end publications from top publishing houses miss some small things. Strive for perfection but don't be crippled by it. Books are works of art, just like any other creation.

Sometimes you can see the brushstrokes. I'm sure I've left a few in this book.

BIG DECISION TIME

By now, you truly hold something lovely in your hands. This is no longer a rough draft. This is a carefully crafted story, fine tuned and polished. It's time to decide what to do with it.

Traditional publish

The good thing about being traditionally published is you have professionals on your team. They will take your polished manuscript to their editors and proofreaders and find a few missed things. A professional formatter will lay it out on the page and create an ebook. An artist will design your cover art and possibly some interior art. A cover formatter will design the cover using that art. The publisher will take care of publication, including handling your BISAC, ISBNs and other pesky details. You sign your contract, sit back and relax.

But don't relax too much. You will most likely still need to do all your own marketing. Publishers have many books to take care of. They want your books to sell, but they want everyone's books to sell and they will focus most of their resources on the books that bring them a return on their investment. If you are marketing your own books as well, you are helping them help you. You will also be sharing all your sales with the publisher and you will have very little say in many of the details.

Self publish

You might also choose to self-publish. In this case you have all the control and you get all the money. You also have to pay for all the proofreaders, layout, art, cover formatting and still do the same amount of marketing, but without the help of a publisher. If you can learn to do many of those tasks yourself, you can save a lot of cash, and make money providing these services to others.

Serial publish

Relatively new on the publishing circuit are serial publishers like Kindle Vella, Radish, and Wattpad. You publish your book by chapter, and readers pay to read on. Usually the first three chapters are free to read and then readers purchase tokens to spend on more chapters. I've heard romance and paranormal romance do very well in this format. I wrote *Soft Deadlines*, a paranormal romance, just to try it. So far it's doing well. I've received payments from it and I only have the first six chapters up.

Serial publishing itself isn't a new concept. The Sherlock Holmes stories by Sir Arthur Conan Doyle were weekly newspaper installments, and there's a reason *David Copperfield* by Charles Dickens is so long. It was all created in serial installments from May 1849 to November 1850. The longer Dickens could keep the story going, the longer he made a paycheck. The prevalence of cell phones and reading apps has given this old trend new life. To publish with serial apps, you will really just need a simple cover image and your marketing. You'll want to target your marketing toward the newer social medias like TikTok.

Visual Novels

Very new on the scene are visual novels. Two popular ones are *Arcane* or *Choices*. A visual novel looks a lot like a game, but the reader has limited ability to choose the story direction. The choices may be to go through the left door or the right, but in the end the next step will carry to the predetermined next part of the story.

To do this you'll need some basic technical knowledge, art and you will have to write your book in a different format. It's doable, however, and turns it into a separate but related work the same as a screenplay can be based on a novel. This means, if you go this route, your visual and traditional novels will be working together to cross market each other.

Audio Production

Audiobooks have been outselling regular print books for a while, and our busy lifestyles can be blamed for the boon. We community, walk, work out, clean house... and listen to books. Producing an audiobook isn't easy and expensive. It's not just an author reading their work. Specialized equipment is involved, sound booths are really necessary unless you like in a cave and it's exhausting. Once the reading part is done, you need to produce it.

Fortunately, you can go through a company like ACX and have your audiobook distributed audible, Amazon and iTunes. ACX is an Amazon company. You can choose to pay a producer up front, produce it yourself or share royalties with an audio producer through ACX and reduce or even eliminate your out of pocket expenses.

I don't see a lot of cons with producing an audiobook with ACX. With royalty share options you can have your book audio professionally produced and sold in all the right channels. You'll still have to market it yourself, but that's no different from your other options.

As I prepare to hit publish on this book in January 2024, KDP has just announced their Audiobooks with Virtual Voice Beta program. It's worth noting that the field of digital publishing and related technologies is rapidly evolving, and companies like Amazon (which owns KDP) are continually developing and testing new tools and services.

Using virtual or synthetic voices to create audiobooks is a growing area of interest in the publishing world. This involves using advanced text-to-speech (TTS) technology to generate audio narration for books, rather than recording human narrators. This significantly reduces the cost and time involved in producing audiobooks which aligns with broader trends in digital publishing:

1. **Accessibility**: Virtual voice technology can make it more feasible for a larger number of books to be converted into audiobooks, increasing accessibility.
2. **Cost-Effectiveness**: Producing an audiobook with a human narrator can be expensive. A virtual voice system could lower costs, making audiobook production viable for more authors and publishers, especially independent and smaller scale ones.
3. **Quality and Customization**: The quality of TTS has improved

significantly, with some systems offering a range of voices and emotional inflections. However, they may still lack the full expressiveness and nuance of a skilled human narrator.

4. **Rights and Royalties**: A virtual voice system could alter the traditional model of rights and royalties associated with audiobook production.

While this is an exciting development, authors should consider the potential trade-offs in terms of quality and audience reception when deciding between human-narrated and AI-generated audiobooks. As of this writing I've created five audiobooks using KDP's Virtual Voice. I considered quite a few factors before I agreed to participate in the program.

One of the first things I considered was all the anger toward AI generated work. I want to make it clear that the Virtual Voice isn't AI at all. AI implies 'intelligent' creation. Virtual Voice is reading back words I created. It's a mechanical voice narration for words I created from my own brain. It's also not nearly the quality of human voice narration.

The second thing I considered was taking income away from an industry. I don't think this holds much water. The truth is most of us can't afford to have an audiobook produced. My husband is actually a voice actor and audiobook narrator and *I* can't afford him. He was just paid over $5,000 to do a project for a private organization. Even though we're married, I can't expect him to take time away from jobs like that to work for me for free.

The books I'm testing KDP's Virtual Voice out on are books I published years ago. If I could have afforded audio on them then, I would have. According to Amazon, only 4% of books get audio treatment. I would think that 4% are the bigger writers. My hopes for KDP's Virtual Voice is that this development will open up new opportunities for the little authors, which is the large majority of us.

After testing KDP's Virtual Voice, I do prefer a human voice over the virtual narrator. For now, I can hear the robotic qualities in the narration but they don't hurt the story for me. Virtual narration is not the best, and now I know that because I've tested it. Bottom line, on my writer budget my options are no audiobook, or a program like KDP's Virtual Voice.

Promotions, Reader Magnets and Loss Leaders

Sometimes your best value isn't in dollars. There's a reason why Costco and Sam's Club lose money on their gas and rotisserie chickens. It's called a loss leader, meaning something to lead people into your place of business in hopes they will buy something else. You may come in for the chicken, but you will most likely pick up a few more things on your way out.

The same can be true for this novel you've just created. If you have a series, offer the book that begins it free if people will sign up for your newsletter. Even if you offer it free with no strings attached, anyone who enjoys the story will most likely go purchase the rest to continue. It also advertises you, builds your reputation and opens doors. You go from being another author hawking a book to someone giving a gift. Best part, ebooks cost you nothing to give away. Whether you distribute 100 or 100,000 it costs nothing. You are definitely receiving though. Advertising costs. Free gifts don't.

You will still have to do all the work of publishing with editors, proofreaders, layout, art, cover formatting and marketing, but your rewards will return in exposure. Just make sure your gift is worth giving. I don't know how many times I've shared this and have an author respond with "I have the perfect thing. I have this one story I could never sell. I'll give that away." No. Just no.

Whatever you are giving away should be your *best* work. Reuse something you have already published that did well. This reader magnet is meant to share your brilliance with the world. People won't be fooled even if it is free and it will still be advertising you, just in the wrong way. You don't want that. If you do use something you can't sell as your giveaway, don't be mad at me when it brings you no returns.

And example of a good free download is a book I wrote with Lee Murray called *Mark My Words: Mark My Words: Read the Submission Guidelines and other Self-editing Tips.* It's a book of our combined notes for a class we taught twice for the Horror Writer Association's Horror University. What started out as a handout grew to be a 50,000 word instruction manual for how to surf the slushpiles and boost your chances to get published.

Every time we teach a class, we give that book away for free as a PDF. In the first year I imagine we distributed hundreds of copies. Despite giving it away, we frequently wind up with sales from it. It boosts our professional reputations and it helps people get to know us and find us. The best part? It's actually a very useful book full of clear information and includes insight from dozens of other publishers and editors in our field. It's a win-win.

II

Building Sales

The following section covers my notes gathered from over a decade on how to build successful promotions using unconventional platforms like Second Life. The information was tested out and refined on my first fiction novella End of Mae.

Using the following methods I managed to bring in an average of $50 USD a month in royalties on that book while I promoted it. At the time, I was disappointed with the results but now I realize as a brand new author just breaking into fiction, that was pretty good. As I find new information, I share it in my weekly newsletter, Authortunities, which is free to read at authortunities.substack.com.

Much of this was compiled from workshops I've taught. I hope you find it useful.

14

How I Got Into This

On 31 May 2011 I published my first book, called, appropriately enough, *End of Mae*. This book was written and published for a few unconventional reasons;

- I had some different ideas for marketing I wanted to try.
- I wanted to write a book about my different ideas.
- I needed something to try my ideas out on.

Thus *End of Mae* was born, my personal experiment to prove that marketing needs a creative mind more than money, and any decent book can be a success with the right marketing. This is truer today than ever before, thanks to the internet which is truly the last great frontier waiting to be conquered.

The beauty of virtual space is that it levels the playing field. In cyberspace you don't need a degree, to weigh 98 pounds, to be blonde, tall, have six pack abs or drive an expensive car. The internet allows us to directly take our personalities and talents and directly profit from them.

Imagine a world where you want to be a star and tell everyone a message. In the physical world you would quickly be arrested leaving graffiti about your pet project on the front of people's property, but in chat rooms and blogs that behavior is welcome and even appreciated. Your attention makes them more valuable property, and their exposure spreads the word about your project.

The win-win situation created by this situation transforms your need into a beautiful, cooperative situation, a true renewable resource. Like love, the more you give the more you will receive. Learn to navigate through the various facets of life online and you learn how to manipulate the virtual universe.

This is the story about the *End of Mae*. Please don't mistake it *for* the story of *End of Mae*, the only vampires and demons you will find in the following pages are my marketing minions. This is the tale behind the tale; the story *End of Mae* was born to live.

15

Make It Your Baby

I don't know how many times I have heard someone confess to me that they "aren't much at promoting". Typically this statement comes from an individual who has created something that the rest of the world would enjoy, but they keep it to themselves as if they are ashamed. In the last few months I've personally asked dozens of published authors what their marketing plan was, and in every case they answered either that they didn't have one, or they mentioned asking for reviews.

Creative people are notoriously inefficient self promoters. The act of creation is so personal to most of us we shy away from 'commercializing' it, taking the term 'promotion' to be synonymous with 'cheapening' or 'selling out'. In some cases this may be true, but if you can't get the news out, essentially you are cheating the world of something wonderful.

Think of any great artist, Mozart, Degas, David Bowie... if they had kept their talents all to themselves, what good are they? The world would be a pale and empty place without the creative element texturing our experience of it. They say it's not what you know, but who you know; and I'd like to take that statement further by saying it doesn't matter who you know, but who you tell.

Creative people can't look at their work as an imposition. If no one likes it, granted, maybe you should keep it more as 'art for art's sake'. The large majority of wonderful creations languish, however, simply because nobody knew about them.

As John Locke points out in his popular book *How I Sold 1 Million eBooks in 5 Months*; "How is it that self-publishing is the only business where self-funding is considered undignified?" If we can't be enthusiastic about ourselves, who else will be?"

I had to change the way I looked at my own work to be able to move ahead with enthusiastic promotion. Your work is your child born in mental anguish. Here's the process I use to help me get over the natural reluctance that comes with promotion. You just have to change your perspective and be a family to your creation.

STEP ONE: LOVE IT LIKE A MOTHER

You have something you want everyone to know about. It may be your blog, your favorite charity, your book, your daughter's modeling career, or your new awesome YouTube video. Whatever it is, it doesn't matter. The principles are the same.

I am marketing a vampire book, a real challenge in the current over saturated market. If my techniques can work to birth another work of fiction into the world with some success, they will definitely work for your pet project. The best part of the deal is I specialize in extremely smart and thrifty marketing, so whatever ideas you use from this book will benefit you without breaking your bank.

The old adage that you have to spend money to make money is has been rendered obsolete with viral marketing. Now with Facebook you can farm friends, Twitter allows you to be the little bird in everyone's ear, and Second Life allows to you enhance your first life... and all from your computer. There is one thing you absolutely cannot afford to have if you want to succeed though; self depreciation.

The biggest turn off for others is usually our attitude. We have an inner voice whispering to us all the time, putting us down and warning us of impending failure. I think this voice comes from our parents, particularly our mothers. Your mom does not want to see you fail, and when you were small she probably spent a lot of time warning you to be careful.

This is good. It keeps you from being burnt by hot grease, kidnapped by strangers and bitten by dogs. It can also keep you standing on the sidelines when you want to be in the center. It limits you and puts safe hedges around you. Your mom's well intended message was *"stay safe."* You did, and you made it to now. Congratulations! Now let's play big kid games.

The first thing you have to learn, before you try any of the things in this book, is to see yourself through your mom's eyes. You listened to her as you grew up; now look at yourself with her glasses on. You aren't suddenly perfect, but I bet all the glaring faults you thought you had aren't so bad. Mothers see us as we should see ourselves, not perfect, but perfect enough.

We aren't expected to do everything correctly. Mistakes are opportunities. Your faults can also be benefits if you look at them correctly. Now look at your pet project with those same eyes. You need to see your baby. Moms are vicious promoters when it comes to their babies. If you want your baby to succeed, you need to stop feeling like you are putting people out and being annoying. This is your baby; you have to show the world how wonderful it is. Hell hath no fury like a woman scorned, and I pity the fool that doesn't admire a doting mother's child. *Learn to be the doting mother of your project.*

STEP TWO: TELL IT LIKE A GRANDMA

Whenever I get on Facebook or check my emails, there's always a stack of messages from a wonderful group of friends I like to think of as my Grandmas. Photos of 5th grade art shows, blog posts written by aspiring teenagers, amusing anecdotes about what they have accomplished recently all waved around eagerly, and each is the most important on the list. I love these messages. They are all examples of marketing at its simplest and purest. They spring from genuine pride and love, and the purveyors of are so in love with their subject matter that you can't help but to start loving it too.

How many people reading this book have picked up a gift for a neighbors child, a co worker's baby, admired a crayon scribble pinned to a wall and bought cheap chocolate bars for <insert sport here>? We all have, because the 'marketer' was so enthusiastic and unashamed of their topic they brought us into their enthusiasm.

On the opposite side of that coin, have you ever been chatting with someone that made self depreciating remarks about themselves, and you realized that your desire to be involved with them was sliding down the scale along with their remarks. The more they downplay themselves, the more you believe and discount them. This is not modesty, it's fear. Sometimes it seems safer to reject yourself before someone else does.

In the beginning, I felt that way about *End of Mae*. Back when I was first trying to design the cover I wrote a funny (I thought) blurb on the back cover. I was embarrassed that I would publish this book, and everyone would utterly ignore it. My blurb discounted myself and basically told anyone reading it, '*Gosh, I so appreciate your charity by even taking interest in this. I completely understand if you don't want to read it. Let's laugh about it together.*'

When I read what I had written to Mr. Smith he was silent, and then he said, "You must really hate this book." I was shocked and denied it, but after rereading what I had written I realized that my 'wit' was just a case of the primary school 'I'll hit you before you hurt me.' I had to look at my book through a mother's eyes and think like a grandma. *End of Mae* wasn't perfect, but she was the best I had made and I needed to be proud of her.

STEP THREE: DISCIPLINE LIKE A DAD

That being said, we all know how unpleasant children that run off into the world with no discipline are. They are rude, insensitive and think only of themselves. This is not what you want your book to be. Before you let it out of the house you have to make sure it's dressed properly and has wiped all the 'clown makeup' off its face.

Dads are traditionally known as the disciplinarians in any given family unit. You must raise your work with strict standards. *Spare the edit, spoil the book* should be in the Bible somewhere because it is absolutely true. Too much of a hard hand squelches creativity in children and artistic creations, but too little produces wild things that don't make sense and no one wants around.

A curious thing about the recent 'eBook revolution', as I hear it being called. The power to publish has been placed in the hands of anyone with basic computer skills. Some tout this as the end of the traditional publisher and they envision lighting the slush piles into bonfires of protest. Some say that the influx of independent authors is killing the market as eager readers get tired of buying garbage.

I personally think that it will all level out. Hopeful indie authors will realize that they aren't going to get famous by quantity over quality. Ultimately the readers will decide, and the long abhorred slush piles have simply moved off the editor's desks and out into the open where anyone can have a go at them. Deregulation just puts the burden of regulation on the individuals involved, the indie creators; otherwise we will descend into anarchy. Here's a recent post I did on the subject;

The Problem with Indies?
  Posted on August 5, 2011

Recently I was discussing the influx of independent authors on the book publishing scene with a friend and I stated that if I were offered a publishing contract right now I'm not sure I would take it. "Why share what I'm already doing?" I asked.

She made some very interesting points in defense of small press publishing, the most compelling being that a large influx of unregulated authors also meant a lot of books floating around with poor editing and rushed plots.

That all too common scenario is actually downgrading the indie scene, creating prejudice towards self published authors. I have known of people who will bypass indie books, however worthy, after getting burnt by a few bad ones.

I've been so caught up in the spirit of literary independence that I hadn't thought about the negatives that accompany a lack of regulation. I do know I've read some books that had so many basic errors that your average high school English teacher would have failed them, and letting these slip through the crack hurts us all. As writers we are making an unspoken promise to entertain, reneging is not an option.

I will be the first person to tell you that my own book is not perfectly edited. If I had the money to pay for editing it at the time, I would have. When I publish the 2nd edition of it, it will be professionally edited. I did use what I had on hand, which was me reading it and editing until my eyes glazed over. I originally published the beginning on Gather.com and got excellent critiques from other writers. In all I think I did okay; out of all my reviews I have only two three star ratings as my lowest, but it could have been better.

As indie authors it's up to us to uphold the standards of our industry as best we can. We must be painstaking in our publishing, weeding out typos and plot errors relentlessly. We must be cruel with our work, holding it to ridiculous standards. End of Mae lost the entire story arc of one of the beginning characters and the sole sex scene during my final chops. It felt terrible to cut out a third of the book and basically toss it in the garbage, but it needed it.

The way I see it, independent authors have two clear paths to take;

Stay independent and be the CEO of your own industry. Learn to outsource tasks you aren't proficient in and master all the rest, including marketing and distribution. Be a professional in every sense of the word. Readers will vote with their dollars and as you continue to plug away publishing new work your reputation as a solid author will establish you.

Start independent and solicit a publisher as your work becomes known. With a press name behind you, I think it does validate you as an author much easier than staying indie. In addition, the publisher takes care of all the business end of book writing and allows you to settle back and focus on production.

Both paths have their benefits and pitfalls, and I don't think there can be a blanket 'best way' statement made. Some may be best suited to go completely rogue and others do best with backing. While I am undecided at this time, being wholly independent may be the direction I eventually take.

I'll have to wait and see what happens. One thing I have found in my two months of being published is that I've entered an industry in the midst of a *revolution. The literary sky flashes with the flames of the burning bourgeois and the masses run a muck. Some scream liberty with blood in their eyes while others cling to staid establishment. Whatever the outcome, it is an exciting place to be... as long as I don't see a guillotine.*

Before we travel on to the marketing techniques that I have been testing through *End of Mae*, I hope you will take a few hours to spend time with what you want to promote and see why it is a gift to the world. If you can't find any reason why, then you should probably go back and give it some loving discipline.

If your project is truly finished and you can love it like a mother, share it like a grandma and give it some good fatherly discipline then let's go on and introduce your baby to the world.

16

Virtual Worlds, The Last Great Frontier

I magine a world where you can do anything. You can create what you think. Distance means nothing; you can communicate with someone on the other side of the world, anyone, just by knowing their name. The limitations of traditional communication are gone. The rules of traditional *everything* are gone. You are now, for all intents and purposes, a god of this world.

This world, and many like it, is as close as your computer. Virtual worlds exist and are incredible tools for enhancing traditional existence. Collectively referred to as the metaverse, there are a plethora of virtual worlds to choose from. The one that I have run my marketing tests on is called Second Life, but any of these worlds could be used in similar fashion to recreate my promotions for *End of Mae*.

Just to give you a sense of the sheer amazing power of this largely overlooked resource, let me give you a few verifiable facts that resulted within the *first month* of my book release.

- Nearly 500 bloggers, magazine editors and other media specialists were contacted with a virtual press release. The entire thing cost under $1 and took me a total of about two hours from start to finish. Press release included promo shirts for girls and guys that could be shared, a replica of the actual book that contained the first chapter among other things.

- Since the press release 30 to 50 new people have visited the End of Mae Virtual Visitor Center in Second Life daily. This doesn't count revisits, the counter I use counts only unique visitors.
- As a direct result of the virtual press release, my virtual location became an editor's pick for Second Life's *Destination Guide*, exposing the book information to 150,930 (and growing) Facebook fans alone.

This is incredible exposure for anything, especially a one month old new fiction. This was done with minimal to no cost. I did have some specialized equipment, such as a virtual printing press to make and distribute the promotional version of my book, but even if I had to purchase that for this project the entire cost would have been well under $20 USD.

The beauty of virtual promotions is that they tend to have two traits that make them priceless. The first trait is that they tend to go viral. You can create a free shirt, add your web address to the description, and pass it out. If you allow it, other people can pass it out to their friends, who can also pass it on. One shirt spreads and replicates itself faster than compounding interest, constantly promoting you.

The second wonderful trait of virtual promotions is the cost, or lack of. You can create a shirt for free, and even if you go all out and purchase templates and textures you *might* spend $10. You can use the same materials to make dozens of different styles. You don't pay another thing, even when that shirt turns itself into 100,000 other shirts. Pixels replicate freely, and for free.

I don't want to mislead you as to how easy this is. It still takes work, dedication and emotional risk. The difference is that for the same cost and stress of say, putting out a press release for your local paper, you can do the same thing better for 500 publications. To give you a true sense of what a virtual campaign looks like, I will now tell you part of the story behind *End of Mae*.

First, know this: I am not new to cyberspace. I met my husband online, and together we started House of SilverJinx, a clothes business in Second Life. To this end I had a large collection of tools for designing clothes, as well as promotional tools such as the ThincPress book printer. In addition, we had owned a large piece of property at one time where we ran rental units and a club. This means a lot of experience with building, designing and working in virtual worlds. Any of the things I have done can be replicated by anyone with a minimum of cost and effort, or can be done by a virtual marketing company for very reasonable cost. I have references and contacts listed in the appendix.

I began my marketing campaign long before *End of Mae* was actually published. I kept a list of notable media contacts I ran across as well as copies of any virtual magazines I came across. One invaluable trick for finding contacts is to read everything with the thought of how can you use this to promote your project. When it came time for me to launch my promotion, I had a ready made list of key people to contact.

When *End of Mae* was published, I knew the real work was about to begin. The first thing I wanted was an interesting base of operations. I decided to create the scenes from the book in a virtual environment. Heylel's mansion took me three days to put up. It contains key scenes from the book, including the dining room, the staircase Mae falls down, the basement and her bedroom. I'll discuss this in more detail later. I called it the End of Mae Virtual Visitor Center.

After the Visitor Center was finished, I asked my daughter to create a trailer to promote the book. It turned out beautifully; featuring the beginning of the book, it gives the viewer a teaser of the story. I actually had a response from one individual that claimed they were purchasing the book to find out "what happens to Mae" and asked if the pixel avatar in the video was "really Mae".

The entrance to the Visitors' Center is set to be an information area. There is the virtual edition of the book set out for passerby to page through, free gift items and other pertinent information. There is a mailbox where people can leave notes for the author, as well as framed pictures up announcing that the site was featured in Second Life's *Destination Guide* and a link to the machinima trailer as well as where to purchase it.

Visitors can travel through the house and interact with the scenes. They can lie in Mae's bed, turn the fireplace on and off and sit in the chairs. This serves to raise questions in potential reader's minds. As they explore, they can wonder why the wine is spilled on the tablecloth and what the big black room with nothing but a spotlight is for. For readers familiar with the tale it solidifies the story in their minds, and makes it easy for them to share the experience with their friends.

After I had my interesting base of operations, it was time to let everyone know. Putting together my press release was a simple affair, and as I said, very low cost. The equipment I used was the ThincBook Press and the Artizan Mailbox system (see appendix). I created everything myself using templates and my own original artwork. In Second Life you can share things in a document called a note card, and you can place photos, landmarks (like portable teleports) and objects of clothing in with the text.

I wrote up my note card press release and added the landmark to the Visitor's Center, a photo of the book cover art as well as some promotional shirts for men and women (as well as matching *End of Mae* panties for the girls) Along with the note card I included my promotional book. Besides containing the complete first chapter of the story, it has a personal message from the author and prompts the reader to visit endofmae.com to find out more. As I said, I dropped this package to around 500 editors, bloggers and fashion bloggers. In addition, around 300 specifically fashion bloggers got a modified press release that focused more on the free clothes items. I released the information myself in a well read fashion blog that I sometimes guest post for (Look What the Cat Brought).

This alone has brought in, as I said, 30 to 50 new visitors every day to explore my book area. The counter I use only counts visits from new individuals and only if they stay for a set amount of time. As I come in to check the traffic counts, there are always people in the area now, paging through the book that is set out and visiting the website. I try to stay out of the way, but today I ran into a visitor that stated she was downloading the book on her Kindle to find out "what all this is".

Having an interesting and interactive base of operations opens up limitless ongoing promotion possibilities. Once a month I try to have a celebration party that features live music, an art exhibit and a live reading from my book.

These parties always feature a live music performance that finishes with an informal Q&A with the author and a short reading in a recreated scene.

The party is always recorded and released as part of the promotion and serves to populate the future parties and potential readers in a number of ways. People love dressing up and coming to the party so they can be 'in the movie'. They and the musician show the video to all their friends, post it on their focused etc. Finally, the video itself raises curiosity about the story, and presents it as more of an experience then 'just another vampire fiction'.

There is so much potential open in this location. I offer an interactive tour that leads visitors through different scenes using landmarks and quotes from the book. Fan art shows can be held there, fashion shows, classes and seminars, live readings and there will possibly be a club on location at some point. Readers and fans have a place to 'hang out' and interact, find out the latest news and pick up new promotional gifts. But what can you offer besides books, shirts and undies? The most important thing you can give is an experience with you.

Here's a blog post I wrote after one of the beginning parties:

One Crazy pARTy!
Posted on August 1, 2011

That was one crazy pARTy...!

From wardrobe malfunctions, stream issues and mass booted guests we had just about every issue we could down to the entertainer, Eric Sweetwater, losing all his internet for about 10 minutes.

In a way tho, it was the perfect indie party. The idea of the whole celebration was to recognize artists that forge ahead on their own, developing their talents and seeing where they will lead them. Indies struggle against lack of resources, faulty equipment and their own self doubts and yet still manage to keep going. It's this spirit of resilience that we were honoring; how appropriate that a spirit of resilience was needed at the pARTy ;p

It was so much fun tho. My Fair iLady got a crash course in virtual partying. Some old and dear friends showed up and I met some new ones.

The music was awesome, the chat stayed lively and I got to experience trying to read in the dark at 6am with no coffee. I wondered if I would be able to enunciate without being properly caffeinated... but it went off well.

Thank you for all that attended... It was a blast seeing everyone. I hope we'll have the video up soon, and we'll do it again next month. Every time gets better and better! xox

17

Your Virtual Tool Box

Understanding what you have to work with allows you to come up with your own unique ways to use virtual worlds for your marketing campaign. There are many helpful videos on YouTube, tutorials and articles and I've included links to some of the best in the appendix of this book. You can build just about anything you need with practice and understanding of the basic principles.

All things in Second Life are made of three elements; prims, scripts and textures.

Prims are the building blocks. You create them in basic shapes, and combine them to make things as complicated as fine jewelry and as simple as a box. They are manipulated in a number of ways and can be shaped, called sculpted prims or giant, called mega prims. They can also be made to glow and have different properties such as phantom (having no physical substance) or physical (can be dropped and manipulated by anyone) among other things.

Textures are the colors and patterns added to make your prims look realistic. You can purchase textures and find hundreds of them for free. You can make custom textures in Photoshop and similar programs. A texture is basically a picture that is added to your prim to bring it to life. Alpha textures are textures that make a part of something transparent. Common uses for alpha textures include windows, lace and holes.

Scripts are what give things the power to perform functions. Scripts use

Linden Scripting Language, or LSL code, brought into Second Life. When added to your prims they can enable them to perform functions. They can speak messages, play sounds, open web pages, give items, explode and any other functions imaginable. You can purchase scripts, find them free or learn to create your own.

Now that you know the basics we can go on. Again, this book's purpose isn't to teach you basic building skills. Those resources are all over the web. Now that you know the lingo I can tell you how to use them effectively. There are links in the appendix for further exploration.

PROMOTIONAL ITEMS

This area is as limitless as your creativity and ability. Not only is there almost no limit on what you can offer, there is a large population of what are known as 'noobs' that are eager to snap your promotions up. These are residents of Second Life that haven't found jobs in world yet (yes, many people hold down actual jobs there) and therefore have limited access to funds. Not only do they flock to get your item, but they tell all your friends before running back into the metaverse sporting your logo.

Besides just clothing items, you can offer footwear, cars, planes, houses and specialty items that support your theme. One of the items I've offered was "Bea's Box", which is basically a refrigerator carton that is referred to at the beginning of the book. When someone drops the box they can get inside and 'play Mae'. Special outfits from the book are also offered at times, such a wine stained dress that Mae wears in 'before and after' versions.

If you are light on creative ability, there are a number of builders available that would be happy to create items for you for a low cost compared to what you'd find outside your computer in the 'real' world. They may be willing to do it in exchange for a copy of your book, or for the artistic credit.

There are also a large number of items available that are classified as "full perm". Sometimes a builder will release wonderful items free and with full permissions for others to modify, copy and redistribute as they wish. These items are being offered 'full perm' meaning that others can do what they wish with them, including modify for their own promotional use.

For example, my husband has a wonderful Mustang styled car in world, full perms. It works the best of any car I have driven in Second Life. Because it's full perm, I can slap my *End of Mae* artwork on the side and use it in promotional machinima, give it away as a prize for a fan art show or just give it to everyone freely. If I so chose, I could resell it, but that wouldn't be as valuable as using it as a promotion.

VIRTUAL PRESS RELEASES

To make virtual press releases, you do not need any special equipment at all. You simply need names to send to. Make a note card up and send it to whomever you want via a convenient 'mail slot' available in all profiles. You can drop anything in a similar fashion; furniture, clothes, animations... size and distance is no limitation. I could take a copy of Heylel's house, and then pass it out for everyone to experience on their own property.

The point of a press release is to be noticed and understood, so you want to focus on clarity and creativity. If they can't understand what you are talking about, you will be ignored. If your press release is painfully bland, you will probably still be ignored. Simple and snappy will probably get you the attention you seek. Editors and bloggers are looking for material to cover, and you can benefit each other in a win-win situation. You give them exciting material to cover, and they give you publicity.

Write up your release with plenty of ways for the recipient to explore more and contact you. Include web contact information such as your email and your links. If you have a location in world to refer to, include that landmark right in the note. Make it easy. Every time I have to work hard to dig up more information on someone's project I shake my head. Don't make someone have to work hard to do you a favor.

Once you have a clearly written press release with all your contact and follow up information included, add some sparkle. Giving away free gifts is effective and costs you nothing, and is a continual promotion. Make sure your gift is related to what you are promoting. I gave away a book that was styled to look exactly like my physical book and shirts that featured a small *End of Mae* logo. If I were a musician I might have given away a guitar decorated with my album artwork that played a little clip of my song. A sculptor might give away a free standing simplified piece of their artwork with a link to their online portfolio. Not to keep pounding this message, but you are limited by your imagination.

As of this book's publication Second Life has more than 20 million registered user accounts. Imagine your promotion going viral among them, gaining exposure all over the world while you sleep. Each of these accounts represents a physical person that takes these influences with them into their daily life where they may download your music, purchase your book or explore your shop. Free to you and while you are busy doing things in your first life.

STAKING YOUR VIRTUAL CLAIM

Probably the most expensive thing in my virtual promotional campaign is the land. Creating things is free, but if you do want to have a set place where you can build a center of operations, you have to have some land. I have quite a large piece, more than ample to hold my entire Visitor's Center, plus the workshop that holds all my printing presses and whatnot. This costs me under $20 a month and includes my premium account fee.

For the exposure I'm getting, this is nothing. I'd pay more for a classified ad in my local newspaper. I do pay for my fees out of the clothing business I mentioned earlier, so it's not an out of pocket expense. You can get a smaller plot of land free with your premium membership that would be suitable for an inworld information center or smaller displays. Premium membership is very affordable when you pay a year at a time, coming out to be around $5 a month.

I don't want to get too deep into the how to of owning land, there is plenty of information on the Second Life website under land. If I didn't have the clothes shop paying the bills I wouldn't be as extravagant and would build a one scene area that I would change once a month and still host live readings there.

Having a virtual presence is not a new idea. Gibson Guitars has an interactive park where you can learn about their guitars and get free guitar themed furniture and amps. L'oreal gave away their signature make up looks for your in world character, or avatar, from a giant purse full of their products. The Chelsea Hotel has an exact replica building built in Second Life to demonstrate the destruction of its historical significance by the new owners. The internet reaches every corner of the globe, and with your own piece of cyber land you can show the world your project.

One of the scenes from my own area was a room where Heylel initially meets Mae that consists of utter darkness and a spotlight. A simple idea, but to create that scene physically would have been daunting to impossible, let alone temporary. In Second Life it is an ongoing marketing tool. Visitors can visit it, and wondering at the story behind it they are prompted to explore the book further. Readers can come and replay scenes, take photos and bring their friends.

Having the scenes rebuilt so that visitors can interact with the book is proving to be invaluable as a way to promote conversation about 'my product' without having to be artificial. People ask, what happened in this room? I then tell them about my story. Doing a live reading in an actual scene from the book is a powerful experience that I think more authors will want to take part in. Combining this with the power of machinima turns a book that would most likely be ignored in the insanely competitive world of fiction, into a hook.

If owning your own piece of land seems daunting, you can rent a shop very affordably at locations that cater to artists. There are many benefits to doing this, and I have a second area that I rent at a place called Book Island.

The benefit to renting a shop at a place like Book Island is the community interaction. There are a range of regular events as well as special ones. The community consist of authors at all levels, publishers, editors and illustrators among others. There are communities built to cater to all genres of creation I imagine, and almost all of them will be renting space. I'll go into more detail on Book Island later in another chapter.

USING THE MARKETPLACE

Besides hand dropping your promotional items into resident's profiles, or sending them via a mail system there is another powerful, and free tool to help you; the Second Life marketplace. This is set up similar to Amazon or eBay but there are no upfront fees to use it.

I have my virtual teaser book up there for free; anyone who wants it can send it to themselves or as a gift in Second Life. The real beauty, however, lies in the actual advertisement they let me have. I can add a video, information and a number of photographs, all free. The marketplace is constantly combed over by people looking for free items, and as they come across your ad they can watch your machinima video, go visit your website and explore the photos you've left.

The marketplace is also another way that readers can share your work. It's one thing to tell your friend about a great book you just read, but how much more rewarding is it to be able to actually send them a sample book free that they can experience like a regular paper book? I can tell you from my experience and feedback that it is indeed very satisfying. Our minds interact with virtual worlds the same as they react with our physical world. As the old adage states, seeing really is believing.

CONNECTING TO REALITY

If you are reading this book, you are probably more concerned about people buying your baby in the regular world then how many free promotional items you can pass out. Connecting the loop between the virtual world and the physical one is important. What good are 5 million 'noobs' running around in your logo shirt if none of them come see your wares?

Fortunately there are a number of effective ways to bring people out of the virtual world and into yours. One handy tool is called an URL script. As I said earlier, scripts are what make things perform actions in Second Life. An URL script can be put in an object to link it to any webpage. When someone touches it in world, a window pops up offering the resident to view a new webpage from inside the game.

This is useful in so many ways. When I have a clothes review, I take a screen shot of the review, post it on a flat prim and add an URL script linking to the actual webpage where it's posted. That creates a bulletin board that prompts viewers to go the page on the web. To show off machinima trailers, I use the same concept; a screenshot of the YouTube viewer on a prim and an URL script. When the Visitor's Center was featured in Second Life's *Destination Guide*, a lovely framed screenshot and URL went up. I cropped down a screenshot of the image of my book with a kindle from Amazon.com's page, and then linked it back. There is a frame up of my book cover art linking to endofmae.com.

The URL script is also handy in other ways. For New Years 2011 we gave away a free party mask to advertise our shop. Hundreds of these went out via the marketplace, and all of them had an URL script that linked to our online shop. These masks paraded through parties all over Second Life, and our shop was introduced to hundreds of new residents.

The URL script is your number one way to close the loop between your virtual promotions and your regular world promotions. The beauty of it is it can be included in any prim, and can be placed in clothes, signs, cars, houses. You are a creative individual or you wouldn't be reading this book. Use your imagination to create new ways to use these virtual tools.

18

Networking Opportunities

A big advantage of virtual worlds is the networking opportunities. Authors and artists can comfortably network with fans from the comfort of their own home. Professionals from all over the world can meet and contribute to each other. With much of the world going digital, it makes sense to take our networking that way. To prove my point, I recently ran an experiment to prove the value of Second Life to a non user.

My volunteer was Amy Eye from The Eyes for Editing. A professional editor, Amy had never tried Second Life before. She agreed to come in and set up her virtual networking from scratch. My job was to help set her up, and introduce her to three different professional organizations and see what she thought. I covered the experiment on my blog, angelaysmith.com. Here's one of the first posts on what I called the My Fair iLady Experiment;

My Fair iLady iDentity Revealed
Posted on July 28, 2011

Yesterday I introduced a brave soul that agreed to be my vic... volunteer for my virtual experiments. Today I shall reveal her identity.

In the flesh she is Amy Eye, a professional editor for two publishing houses. She also does freelance editing for writers in her spare time. Visit her website to find out more about her.

In Second Life she is Dranea, the avi with the million megapixel smile. She bravely chose a digital version of herself and with an extraordinary pioneering spirit, logged on. What a hoot that turned out to be. Like a crazy Twilight Zone slumber party we talked clothes and make up... and then went on to try new skins and hair on her iSelf.

Then things got crazy when swarms of artists decided to show up and start setting up their exhibits for August (I'll be introducing the last them before the exhibit starts, don't worry). Poor Dranea was deserted as I ran around like a crazy person, my communication dropping to the level of hurried, half finished apologies. No worries tho, this resourceful woman took it upon herself to reshape her buttocks whilst waiting*.

We didn't get to finish all our pixel primping in that session, but Dranea is coming back to see her first Second Life social gathering, the big Indie pARTy being thrown down this Sunday. I can't wait to see how she likes meeting and chatting with artists, musicians and writers (oh my!) from all corners of the globe. THEN we'll be setting her up with her own virtual editor shop on Book Island... after we recover from the festivities anyways.

This experiment is to show how beneficial Second Life is for those who need some panache for pennies. From networking in professional organizations such as the MWGA to socializing, it's all here. Amy is new to Second Life and will be offering her unbiased opinion of the experience. If she says it's a waste of time I will concede that perhaps I am crazy.

If she agrees with me tho, I expect every indie artist/author/musician that needs exposure (that's all of us) to run to their computer and literally jump in. I will even hold classes to help set everyone up and do whatever I can to help.

I believe in the indie spirit; it is raw creativity, belief in one's own gifts and a mind open to any challenge. Indie is not a title to fling around lightly, it is a way of life. Second Life enhances it perfectly.

* Reason Second Life is great; free, non surgical body enhancements anytime you want._

Amy Eye is enjoying getting to know Second Life in a business sense. As she says;

"Second Life is really something I am more and more interested in every time I learn something new that I can try out in this virtual world. At first, all of the menus, the files, the environment, and figuring out where you belong can seem a bit daunting, a bit overwhelming. I came from a gaming background, so I was less afraid of opening up menus and playing around with things until I either figured it out or found someone who could explain it to me.

The best suggestion that I would give to anyone starting out in Second Life: Don't give up. There are some amazingly kind, talented, helpful, and resourceful people in Second Life. Many of them are more than willing to give a hand to a 'Noob'.

This environment could really help my editing business by introducing me to many authors and getting to know them prior to needing my services. By the time they would be looking for en editor, we will already have background knowledge of each other and will know if we will work together well or not. Not only is Second Life a unique place to network, but it is also a fun place to be. I went to a social gathering recently and the music and the art on display were breath-taking as well as marvelously done. There is a whole second world out there waiting to be explored and utilized."

Amy is enjoying her Second Life experiment, and proving that the platform is a viable resource for serious business. But what of this Book Island that we set her shop up on?

As I mentioned in previous chapter, Book Island is a virtual community of writers, publishers and anyone else having to do with the industry. For just a few dollars a month you can rent a shop space. Your shop can display your advertisements, link to pertinent websites and serve to promote you any way you can imagine. You can also arrange to do regular readings there, live question and answer sessions and greet fans.

My own shop passes out free gifts that promote my books, links to my Facebook fan pages and all the places my books are for sale as well as my blog. The top floor is a smaller version of a scene recreated from *End of Mae* that

I have up at my Virtual Visitor Center. It gives me the power to do smaller more intimate readings of that scene.

Book Island is also great for networking with other writers. One of my favorite activities is attending the live readings. Creativity is welcome and authors can come in as their characters to do readings as anyone or thing they choose. The first reading I ever attended was called Happy Hour with Habeker Haber, and the author was reading as a giant liquor bottle. The experience was warm, welcoming and full of laughs, but even more importantly it was a valuable network tool. From that first meeting I got set up to do live readings at two other major events. Taking care of business while having fun is the way it's done when you're pixel perfect. To get a sense of some of the shenanigans on Book Island, here is the post I wrote after that first reading;

A Scrabble of Scribblers
  Posted on July 22, 2011

Only on Book Island can you get a Happy Hour reading from a whisky bottle...

  If a group of geese are a 'gaggle' and a bunch of crows are a 'murder,' than what would you call a bunch of writers hanging out? A 'waggle of worders'...or a maybe a 'scrabble'?

  Whatever the official term, that's what I experienced this morning when I attended a reading by the often hilarious and sometimes spooky Hakeber Haber. Afterwards we all sat around chatting, and while the subjects ranged from boobs to veteran hippies, they always had a literary undertone. Seriously, they did.

  I can't remember when I've had more fun with a bunch of fellow scribblers. I'm not a stranger to 'writer's associations' but never have I met such a relaxed and happy group. Something about sitting in the comfort of my own home and having a good laugh over a cup of my own (better than Starbucks) coffee in my bathrobe made the whole experience deliciously indulgent.

  If you are a writer of any kind, you need to get yourself on Second Life *and over to Book Island*. I have met so many great people from all areas of writing and all levels of experience. It doesn't cost money, and you don't even have to brush your hair (I didn't ;p) You will not regret all the opportunities and inspiration that will cascade over you like rain on the desert; utterly surprising, riveting and capable of surrounding you with vibrant life.*

I can see that the biggest problem I will have with Book Island is breaking away from the fun to get some work finished... and speaking of... I must continue with my self-imposed servitude. Ta 'til tomorrow! xox

Book Island was started by Selina Greene back in June 2007. In her own words;

'I had come into SL 6 months previously to market my RL publishing company on a small mainland plot. No-one came, so I thought that if there were more publishers, writers and book-related people around me, more people would visit, especially if we held discussion events. It worked and we decided to hold a SL Book Fair in March 2007. I had gone from a 512m plot to a quarter sim in a couple of months and it was clear there was a demand for more, so I bought a private sim soon afterwards and we all moved to Book Island.

The initial reaction towards Book Island was highly enthusiastic - it was an incredible, magical time in SL for all involved. We filled the sim in a matter of 6 weeks and we had to build more shops to cater to demand. I still have some very fond memories of those early days, propping up that old, ugly wooden bar in the corner of the Writer's Block cafe with other residents, talking nonsense and setting the world to rights. That bar has become somewhat of a historical monument in the island's history and I still harbor the fantasy of making it a gathering point once more. I'm pleased to say that some of our original residents are still on the island, including Arton Tripsa and Diana Allandale.

Book Island was ground-breaking at the time - it was the first dedicated literary sim in SL. Since then, many others have been created and are thriving. I feel that Book Island showed the SL community that it was possible to have a space dedicated purely to books, publishing and writing, which has inspired others to follow suit. Today we have a wonderful network of literary sims who all pull together and do great things.

Book Island is thriving - we have so many events and regular faces at them. It's such an exciting time. As far as tier payment goes, we are completely self funding through the rental of shops and houses. I would underwrite any shortfall on tier, should there ever be one, so Book Island's status is complete secure. We have a few empty shops at the moment, not many, but keeping us 100% full is a bit of a challenge at times. For anyone who has thought about joining Book Island and hasn't, you don't know what you're missing - give it a go!

We have some exciting developments in the pipeline, including the creation of a library of SL books, but really we plan to build on our successes so far rather than changing or radically expanding. We have an amazing community that I'm honored to be a part of and I treasure it greatly.

A presence on Book Island in itself isn't going to be a game-changer in most cases. It takes an effort to market that shop through a classified ad, picks etc. It also takes time to get known and seen, so becoming part of the community helps greatly. That said, I know of copy-editors who have gained a good amount of paid work through their storefronts, I know of authors who have gained RL publishing contracts through their presence of the island from RL publishers who have been on the island too. For writers, there is an opportunity to direct people to free chapters, their website and ebook websites and for publishers to link to Amazon for RL book sales. And, a book island presence is a great thing to brag about in RL marketing plans. The possibilities are endless!"

Book Island is just one of the ways that Second Life can enhance your real life marketing. There is a thriving press community from radio and television to a plethora of excellent magazines. Don't be fooled into thinking that this is 'playing' at business. These publications are professional, sell advertising and are constantly on the lookout for new stories. My first interview when I launched *End of Mae* was The SL Enquirer. I was exposed to their large and established readership and sold more books in that week than I did for the rest of the month.

Lanai Jarrico, the founder of The SL Enquirer let me turn the tables on her and gave me an interview about how she started her publication;

"I started the original virtual world news source The TSO Enquirer (TSOE) on October 4, 2004, while I was exploring another virtual world by the name of The SIMS Online. It was my first real experience with this type of social culture and I was immediately drawn to the chance to meet and socialize with people from all over the country and world in a 3D kind of way. I always liked to explore and interact with the many people I would meet and began to notice different situations that would occurred in the virtual world so I thought I would create a website news source and write about the various things going on.

Soon, TSOE went viral before I even considered being in this field of virtual world journalist. It really was just a mere idea to create a platform for news generated in that virtual world and a place for avatars to express themselves.

My inspiration came from my circle of friends, in one of the cities, called "Blazing Falls". I would visualize myself on a soapbox for my friends, to entertain and inform them of the things going on in The SIMS Online, including Role Play Mafia News. I have to give them credit for their entertaining news contributions. It helps our newspaper grow in popularity.

In early 2005, I was invited to become a member of Second Life by amateur filmmakers; Alain Dellanegra and Kaori Kinoshita. They asked me to be a part of their film project. Alain and Kaori traveled from Paris with their assistant Jean Martin to meet me and work on a documentary project involving virtual world culture.

During their visit, they asked me to join Second Life but I was apprehensive about trying it at first because I had heard it was an adult type of game with lots of sexual content. I was not immediately amused by that and wanted no part. After hearing many of my online friends talking about frequenting this new virtual world, I decided to give it a try, so in May of 2005 I created Lanai Jarrico, the cross-over began and was completed by 2006 when I officially purchased the new www.slenquirer.com domain and made it active.

Virtual journalism was a pretty new type of media when I started and The TSO Enquirer was the leading paper in Blazing Falls. I would say the initial reception of TSOE was welcoming because it was fun and resourceful. Many found it appealing because they were able to express themselves by having their articles published.

Through hard work, friends that encouraged me to continue to do what I do and my passion for writing, I can now say, I am a full time college student with a 3.6 GPA and I am still doing what I do. One thing I learned in media is you must have an extra layer of skin and not allow everyone's opinions to manipulate your own thoughts. I also learned to work with people rather than try and compete. This is where most of the acceptance and trust from our readers comes from today.

When I first began, the biggest challenge was managing the newspaper on my own. I wore all the hats from news production, editing, website design and publishing. As the years passed and our staff began to grow, I was able to create the SLE Family. They are an amazing group of individuals that share a passion for the virtual world and documenting news as it happens. Because they believe in SLE and contribute news, I have to give them credit for making up what it is today.

I See SLE expanding and crossing over into real life news. Because I have witnessed the power of viral advertising and social networking. I see the potential for criss-crossing barriers in virtual world media involving many online businesses, leisure internet users and virtual gamers on a global scale.

Through the years SLE has worked with many different writers, in- world businesses, charities and entertainers that utilize the virtual world to expand on their businesses, self promote and provide entertainment to resident's across the grid. As the virtual world grows and changes, we have to adjust and make changes too. I am happy to continue doing what I do and seeing what new doors open. There are a few new things on the horizon for SLE right now, but you will just have to wait and see what happens next."

I've introduced you to a network of writers, and a virtual magazine, but my introduction to Second Life networking wouldn't be complete without bringing up a network of media, The Magazine Writer's Guide Association (MWGA), an association with an emphasis on improving professional standards and education.

With regular seminars on new developments in the field, MWGA runs a tight ship with disciplined guidelines on participation. The benefits are many from educational seminars to socializing with key media players. What can be more beneficial to an indie author than attending a party with all the major magazines? To explain the benefits of MWGA, I'll include the blog post I wrote just after I began to get involved with this excellent group.

MWGA: Beneficial For Global Media
Posted on June 29, 2011

A recent brainstorming session at MWGA

Networking and diversity are the key factors for media professionals to succeed. The internet has opened many doors, but Skype conferencing can only go so far to establish genuine relationships on a global level. Studies have shown that seeing is believing, especially when it comes to our behavior. Virtual experiences affect the way we react physically.

People who spend time running on virtual treadmills may never break a sweat physically, but their mind perceives the workout and accepts it as real, losing real weight. Those directed to cut down virtual trees in a game wind up making more ecologically sound choices in their physical world.

In business, they've found that sitting in a conference room with business associates from around the world becomes accepted in the mind as much as a local meeting. Relationships are built and respected when the voice has a face, and we can actually dress for success in a virtual environment.

To this end Lyric Navarita started the ™MAGAZINE WRITER'S GUIDE ASSOCIATION, or MWGA. This is a group of magazine editors, bloggers, editors, graphic artists, writers and others dedicated to working together to benefit the group as a whole. Recognizing that there is strength in diversity and cooperation, this is a professional organization that is achieving footholds in Europe, Australia and the US.

The pen is mightier than the sword, and a group of media individuals banded together in unified purpose is an army. Services are available to members from renting the corporate conference rooms for private and business functions to being able to brainstorm with professionals in every aspect of media. MWGA is a valuable resource for all business that needs media, in other words, all business.

Lyric Navarita started the MWGA in the summer of 2010. She started out working alone finding magazines to add to the association. In her own words;

"I have always had a passion for magazines real life as well as on Second Life. There are many associations that people are involved in but I haven't noticed one for magazines or bloggers. This industry is always competing with each other and hardly come together to learn. I thought it would be awesome if there was an outlet where the industry could come together and teach to become better, even in friendly competition. In the beginning no one understood my ideas. I had to rewrite my vision and break it down over and over again. I realized that the only way people will understand is through actions. Therefore, I wrote the overall generic view of the association and set it up where people have freedom of voice. To where they feel as if their ideas contributes towards the direction of the generic vision. After almost a year now, people are just beginning to understand what I was trying to explain to them.

My biggest challenges are teamwork, commitment and financial. Having a good team around me to help expand this group on a international level and getting more members involved more are very important towards our success. People express how much this association is needed and how much they want to get involved - the door is always open. There's a lack of dedication sometimes and many people speak more than they place action towards the words they speak. We are a non-profit association and we work hard volunteering our time and efforts to build this association. I pay for everything and in the beginning that was fine because I was establishing myself. We're at a place now where MWGA has paid their dues and I believe we can start requesting fees from members and non members to go towards continuing this association. If people appreciate what we are trying to achieve then they should be willing to help us keep this up.

We're living in a digital era where everything is computerized. MWGA may have started inside a virtual game on a computer but I plan to trademark it into a real life company once I build a stronger foundation, structure and gain higher numbers. I have long term plans for this association but no real life launch date yet. I'm the process of filing all the necessary paperwork to make this more legitimate. My overall plan for MWGA is to take over the grid on Second Life, become deeply international, and host more educational tools for learning and growth in the industry as a whole."

The organizations and people in these chapters are just a brief taste of the network opportunities available in Second Life. As close as your computer and there's no need for a new wardrobe or even changing out of your pajamas and you can be performing live readings, attending business meetings and interacting with readers. And you will never have a bad hair day unless you want one.

19

Beyond the Virtual Borders

Second Life was an enormous boost to my publicity and sales, but I couldn't have done it in the virtual world alone. I had to be able to transition smoothly between worlds, and the internet cloud makes that easier than ever. One of the most effective ways to close the circle is with your blog. I recently compared my marketing plan to a spider's web. Branches go out in all directions, but tying them altogether to have one coherent purpose is my blog, smack in the middle of it all.

USING YOUR BLOG

In the first year my blog was one of the most valuable tools in my marketing arsenal. To effectively use your blog, start it well before you have a project you want to promote. There are few things more discouraging then trying to get readers for your blog so they can support your pet cause.

Blogging is a little like romance. You can't just buy your readers a drink and expect them to roll over to your demands. If you are trying to market anything, you need to think long term; you want a marriage over a one night stand. While monogamy is great for marriage, when you are thinking marketing you should think like a polygamist. You have to romance multiple readers simultaneously with the skill of a Don Juan that throws phrases instead of roses. Each and every reader must be constantly wooed, because they are gone as soon as your last blog post has been read.

A blog is invaluable for a number of reasons, the most important being it's one of the best ways to establish a relationship with readers. In your personal blog you can become friends, share your personal info and allow your voice to come through. You don't have to be on your polite behavior as you do in guest posts and other writing. Let your hair down and let your readers see the real you. They will love you, and a relationship is born.

Another reason a blog is valuable is because if it well done, it becomes currency. Originally my blog was done on Blogger. I started being prompted to move to WordPress, a 'professional' blogging platform. I will try pretty much anything once, so I moved over. I have not regretted it. I wound up with a sharp looking blog that I have received so many compliments on. Not wanting to spend money on promotions, I've offered to trade services and advertising on my blog, and that has worked out well every time.

Many people get into blogging because they have an idea that you can make a big paycheck for just writing a few posts, and while that may happen, it's not where the average blog will give payback. A blog is your ticket to go places you wouldn't normally be welcomed in. Your blog is your best way to donate and support noble causes, shed light on other artists that need it and help promote other businesses – and it all pays you back directly.

For instance, several times I've seen people asking for support and votes for their different causes. It takes me maybe 10 minutes to screenshot their cause and write a quick "please support this" post to my blog. I send the link back to them and besides being able to give someone a little extra boost beyond my button click, they have always been thrilled, and shared my link with their circle of friends. This brings me traffic and new readers and friends.

I don't advertise on my blog much, unless it is a direct ad trade with someone. When I wanted to find some new places to promote my book I simply asked a few of the larger blogs and publications if I could guest post for them occasionally in exchange for doing posts on them at my website. Every time I've asked the answer has been a yes, with usually more offered than I've asked for. I've been given staff writer positions with the sole assignment of promoting my own interests.

Don't have anything to write about? Create your own great stories. Take your pet project and create activities that make material for you to blog on and promote your activities. This creates a mighty whirlwind of marketing that is unstoppable and definitely attention getting. Here's an example;

I mentioned I have a virtual clothes business in Second Life. I own land, and have a shop that people can roam through. I decided to promote Second Life as a serious way to exhibit art. To that end, I set up art shows in our shop area. The artists were invited to sell their work and place out a tip jars, keeping all proceeds. In addition, I'd write a blog post up on their work, do a slideshow of the exhibit and perhaps a machinima if my daughter had time. Perhaps that seems generous of me, but if considering what I get in return, it's a fair trade.

First, I benefit because the artist will share my post I wrote featuring them proudly with all their professional and personal contacts. That gives me traffic, as well as introducing me to new readers, some of which will stay. Secondly, because the exhibit is sponsored by House of SilverJinx, the virtual clothes store, it also introduces my product line to all their Second Life associates. Because I'm promoting Second Life as a real business tool, I can share it with my virtual business associates.

All of these people are introduced to my book, *End of Mae*, either by seeing it in the sidebar of my blog, or from seeing the free promotional gifts I have set up in my shop. In other words, the exhibit promotes the shop and blog, which promote the book, which promotes the clothes business. The exhibit becomes the catalyst for a marketing whirlwind, and I can do it new every day. There is a plethora of artists, musicians, writers, dancers, designers, magazines… in the physical and virtual world. By helping them out, you help yourself out.

I could go further and sponsor an art show that would exhibit fan art from End of Mae with the prize being gift cards to our clothes shop. This costs nothing for me, and would generate some good promotional material for my blog and social network sites. Artists could get their work exposed. Someone would get a free wardrobe. It's a win-win, my favorite equation.

Make your blog easy to find and easy to read. I've clicked off of too many blogs that had crazy fonts, garish back ground patterns and dozens of advertisements and widgets in the sidebars. It is very helpful to have a domain name to help people find you. At the bottom of each email I send I include my name and a link to my blog. I wish I had a penny for every time I've had to 10 minute search to locate someone's blog. Make it easy for people to find you and when they do, make it simple for them to read you.

I think the secret of a good blog is to see it as a quality jewelry setting. A jeweler creates a basic setting and often uses the same setting repeatedly to showcase the gems he has access to. Your blog should be that setting, simple and distinctive and designed to showcase your gems. The gems are everywhere and grateful to be found. They are your neighbors, friends, teachers, crafters... anyone who passes near you is a potential diamond waiting to be polished with your words and turned into something lovely to share. And, like a jeweler, you will be paid back.

STAR POWER WITH MACHINIMA

If a picture is worth a thousand words, then a video must be worth at least ten thousand. Machinima, or videos created in digital environments, is a way that you can add extra spark to your blog and promote yourself. Think of owning your own movie company that operates on little cost. Actors that will work for free and do exactly what you tell them, backdrops that don't require artists to paint and you can work with people from all over the world with no jet lag. That's the beauty of machinima.

Machinima started out as games were used to create music videos, a sort of techi fanboy/girl activity. Machinima has the distinct advantage of being economical, efficient and easily obtained; three important aspects of any marketing tool.

My own experiences with machinima marketing started as I watched music videos that my then teenage daughter had created. I sat through hours of pelvis grinding warlocks dancing to rave music before it started clicking in my head that these had promotional potential. There are a multitude of games to choose from, giving the machinimist a veritable endless variety of actors and situations that will work for no pay at any hour and at a minutes' notice.

My daughter jumped right on board with the idea, and started pumping out the videos, collecting them on her YouTube channel, Ember Marketing. There you can see a dark elf turn a viral World of Warcraft joke into a promotion for a blog post. She created my book trailer in Second Life, inventing the virtual face of Mae in the process. A popular musician had her create his music video in Second Life for an original song of his.

The most important thing to recognize in the use of machinima as a marketing tool is to keep it quality. Just because you can create a full scale production alone in your basement with a good computer and basic software doesn't mean you can treat your production like a hobby. I don't personally do machinima, believing it to be better left in the hands of someone much more adept, namely, my daughter, so much of this information is courtesy of her.

When she gets ready to do a machinima, a set is built and issues like lighting and special effects carefully considered. She is very careful to avoid infringing upon copyrights and has sources of free domain music and images for what she can't provide herself. She sets herself a deadline, gets what she needs and produces it in good time. The results never fail to capture attention with minimal cost, especially when compared to traditional methods.

The other day I saw an advertisement for a book trailer featuring three still photos ran through PowerPoint offered up for a price of $350. The photos were stock photos, but for an extra fee the creator would use "custom" photos. If the author wanted more slides added there was a "per photo fee" as well as a charge of $500 for anything that used "animated photos." At this time my daughter currently charges $100 for a completely animated trailer that has music and special effects. While her prices will have to go up as the demand for machinima trailers increases, even at the max prices what is more interesting; a PowerPoint slideshow or an animated film production?

For example, my book trailer features the main character, Mae, acting out the opening scene from the book. She is in the spooky twilit woods of New Jersey, and something is watching her from the shadows. It stalks her, changing its viewpoint as it circles in ever closer. Mae huddles next to a refrigerator carton in the shadows, a growing feeling of unease creeping up her spine. She hears a noise and turns to face it, calling out her companion's name as the image blacks out. Threatening sounds cut through silence and are replaced by ominous music. A supportive quote about my book from another author appears, and then smoke washes over the screen and recedes to reveal my *End of Mae* cover, and then where to find it, endofmae.com. It was effective, and I have been told a few times that someone bought it because the trailer was so intriguing. One girl actually asked me, "Is that really Mae?" She was referring to the digital character created to represent Mae, again, seeing is believing.

The use of machinima allowed me to bring the story to life in a new and easily digestible form. The best part is that the very nature of machinima makes it so easily shared and viral. It was ready to go within days of the official book release, and immediately I was able to share it on my Facebook, Twitter, blog, Amazon.com and Smashwords author profile pages, my Gather.com, Goodreads and feature it in my monthly machinima column for Hypergrid Business, to name a very few places. I'm linked to it in Blogcritics articles and guests posts as well.

Because I was sharing machinima with music and entertaining visuals, it was more eagerly accepted than the traditional, "Let me tell you about the new fiction book I just published… wake up!" Not only was it watched and commented on, but the most important thing is that it was *shared*. With a simple click, anyone who enjoyed it could "like" it and share it on their social sites.

I used my URL script to put a link to it in the virtual Visitor's Center, as well as posted it on my End of Mae page on my blog, so it is constantly snaring new viewers which can potentially turn into new readers. The ways to share this gem are still manifesting as well. Recently my husband was watching a YouTube video on the Jersey Devil legend, and he asked why we weren't posting the book trailer as video responses to the hundreds (at least) videos on YouTube of the same subject. It was a "duh" moment for me, and I quickly scribbled it down on my marketing to do list. New ways are still being created on how to use machinima for cost efficient and effective viral marketing, and we are just about ready to create trailer number two.

The flexibility of machinima is as attractive as the lack of cost. To recreate the spooky pinewoods of New Jersey would have been near impossible for us. She was located in Florida and I was in Australia. It would have cost around $5,000 to meet and film on location. Instead, we met in the virtual world of Second Life and went to a public building area known as a sandbox. We had built the set and filmed the entire thing in a few hours. She put it together, added music and effects and I had a book trailer before I would have even been able to clear customs out of Australia.

If you don't already know how to make machinima, you would probably benefit from finding someone who already knows the ropes. The good news is that it may be your kids, or their friends. Machinima is a vibrant visual art form that combines commercialism with the technicolor finesse of Andy Warhol blended with Ninja Turtle energy. It's addictive, flexible and totally viral. The typical first response usually had after watching a good piece of machinima is to share. As someone with something to market, that's exactly what you want.

20

Partner Up

Piggy back marketing is another subtle way to start a marketing whirlwind. That is done best by partnering up with some of the word of mouth marketing sites out there, such as MyBlogSpark (US) and Vibe Village (Aus). These sites work by offering you free products to try, and then you share what you think of the products with your friends and family, as well as writing reviews.

With a beautiful blog at your disposal, you are positioned to benefit from this situation in multiple ways. First off, you get stuff. I'll use my Cadbury Chocolate campaign as the example (one of my personal favorites). I applied for the campaign through Vibe Village, and because I have a pro looking blog with a large readership, I was accepted. Instant benefit, I get a box of chocolate. And it gets better.

I shared my chocolate, introducing the new product to my friends and family. When I passed out the chocolate, I was able to say it was due to my blogging efforts that I was able to give it, reaping positive blog promotion. I took photos relating to the chocolate gifts for anyone that would let me, and shared their photos in my blog and reviews. More promotion for my blog as they shared the posts with their family and friends. To top it off, I took a few photos of my husband eating the chocolate while reading *End of Mae*.

The Cadbury campaign was centered on having what they called 'me time' while enjoying your chocolate treat. The book entered in nicely as a relaxing thing people like to do when eating chocolate. And it just happened to promote my book. So basically, I got paid in chocolate to promote my blog and book to my friends and family, as well as Cadbury, Vibe Village and my readers. Does it get better than that?

Other ways I have seen piggyback marketing used includes my daughter introducing a recipes and video reviews as machinima style as Mae or 'on location' from my Virtual Visitors Center. Big brands have paid billions to give their names credibility, and if you can do it in context, you can piggyback on their marketing quite easily. The companies use word of mouth marketing firms to publicize their products. You promote them to all your fans and yourself to theirs. It's just another win-win situation, with everyone benefiting.

WORD OF MOUTH GOES BOTH WAYS

Word of mouth marketing is not a new concept, but its recent use by the big boys of business is. The basic precept of WOM is that the average consumer has lost faith that corporations really have their best interest at heart. You may be smirking, but just think back to the 50s when whatever the television told people to buy, they bought hook, line and sinker.

Today's consumer isn't so gullible. Years of carcinogenic miracle sweeteners, animal testing exposes and sweatshop disclosures have seen innocence shrivel up and die like yesterday's claims to be eco friendly. Millions of dollars are spent by big business to get your attention, and you have stopped listening. How on earth can they get your attention now?

Fortunately, corporations have found someone you'll still listen to; your friends and family. People have a tendency to want to share good finds with those closest to them. Word of mouth marketing seeks to capitalize on that phenomena, and wisely so. When Coke says that their new diet version tastes the same as the original, we can easily discount that information based on our individual prejudice and experiences. When your work mate tells you they switched to the new Coke based on flavor and lack of calories, you are more apt to listen... and buy.

Big business was quick to note and capitalize on this, to their credit. Why spend billions of dollars on an expensive advertisement when you can give 1,000 people a chance to try your product for free for a lot less? Chances are, a good portion of those people will enjoy the product, and pass it on. Even better if you can get them to blog it, "like" it, Twitter it… That's what word of mouth marketing means to big business, but the excellent thing about anything viral is that it works best from the ground up, and you and I are on the ground.

What you need to use word of mouth marketing to your advantage is a few cheerleaders, people that will settle solidly in your corner and start attracting others. One you have these, the attention you need will start gathering for you as people stop to see what the hubbub is all about. The problem is, getting your first cheerleaders.

Like leaves piling in a corner, seems like one or two brings a dozen and it keeps multiplying from there. The trick is getting the first few leaves to pile up, but that can seem daunting when you are putting your work out there. It's much the same as sending a child off to kindergarten. We have to trust that they will find new friends, but sending some 'first day' treats for their friends goes a long way towards popularity.

The best way I found to get cheerleaders in your corner is to go looking amongst the sympathetic; the other new authors/musicians/inventors/artists. I started being vocal in groups where writers tend to hang out and share such as Goodreads. There's a ton more, but like Mark Twain I believe in putting all my eggs into one basket and watching that basket like hell.

I started building relationships with my fellow new authors and hopefuls. I didn't try to lord over them with superiority, because first, I knew I wasn't superior and second, who wants to help someone that's better than them? I offered help when I could, and as generously as I could. The same was reciprocated. I was honest in saying I needed "likes" for my new *End of Mae* fan page on Facebook. I posted the link, and then stated I'd be glad to "like" and follow anything that someone asked of me in the comments.

I kept these conversations off my Facebook for the most part. That was 'shop talk' and was saved for those of us that were in the battlefield with me. Like soldiers that become like brothers through adversity, we started banding together to support each other socially. It made a big difference. No longer did my posts announcing new book reviews sit unnoticed. When my fellow soldiers saw them, they liked and commented, attracting more of the same.

I also have to say I was blessed by an amazing, supportive daughter. From the beginning, I'd make jokes when I'd get an interview. "Wow, I feel almost famous." I'd laugh. "Mom, you *are* famous!" she'd answer. She liked all my posts, shared with her friends, made multitudes of machinima, gave her opinion, brainstormed ideas… Like any mom, I have been her fan since the day she was born. That she returned the favor has been a gracious blessing. You'll need a head cheerleader for your team, and if you can find one like mine you'll have a huge head start.

Everyone else you'll probably have to ask outright. I made a post on my blog enlisting help. I used the old "I want you" Uncle Sam poster, but I Photoshopped in the words "To share the news". The post basically said the *End of Mae* was going to go nowhere fast if I didn't have help sharing the info. I didn't ask anyone to buy the book, I offered to give it free (in electronic format) to anyone who would be willing to review it.

I also made it clear that I needed publicity, not lies. If the story stunk, tell everyone. I offered to do anything I could to help; do live Q&A sessions, answer interviews, offer free eBooks (free to me also). The response was phenomenal. My info was ecstatically shared everywhere. I got set up for two Q&A sessions for Goodreads, both primarily populated by bloggers and writers. I gave away a free eBook to everyone who asked a question.

In the beginning, word of mouth is more valuable than money. I might have sold a few books during all that, and gotten no publicity. Instead, in the first month *End of Mae* had 20 individual reviews, 4 interviews, 2 Q&A live chats, 2 spotlights and had 2000 unique visitors to the virtual build in Second Life. For what I've seen of first time fiction, that was phenomenal. It wasn't that *End of Mae* was so great; what worked was that it was that it was pretty good, and my marketing plan turned out to be great.

That is a large part of why I was so determined to finish off this book on marketing before I finished off what has now turned into the *End of Mae* series. There are many books out there better than mine, and they are languishing unloved because the author lacks the money and know how to market. This book answers both problems. The only thing you have to do is *do* it.

FAN ART MASTERPIECES

Nothing gathers the fans like fan art. Fan art says to everyone, this isn't just worthy of my attention, this has inspired hours of labor for the love alone. Fan art begets more fan art, and pretty soon you have a whole culture built up around your words, letting the rest of the world know that your work is indeed worthy.

My first fan art was made by my daughter, a very distinctive picture of Mae in Heylel's beam of light. An easily recognizable icon from the story, it proved to be an excellent point of curiosity. Besides being excellent artwork, it was an excellent attention getter. She started an account on Deviant Art, a site for fan art of all kinds, and added my endofmae.com domain to each of her creations so curious viewers would know where to go and find out more.

A second one she did the same night and it showed the two sides of Mae. It was the Mae she had created for the machinima trailer, resting against a wall, looking peaceful. Behind her was a second Mae, looking vicious with fangs. Not only was it not an "official" illustration, which prompted curiosity, but it also raised questions. Why were their two girls, were they twins or two aspects of the same girl. Anything that raises questions about your project is good.

Fan art is valuable in so many ways. Shared on your social sites and blog helps the artist get some feedback and renown as well as showing your appreciation. They proudly show all their friends their featured artwork. In turn, that brings more potential fans to you. I of course shared the art on my blog and social sites, and it got me thinking of how I could get more fan art, and I can see contests coming into play. There is certainly a lot left to discover in this area.

There are places on the internet where writers tend to gather, and one of my favorites was called, appropriately enough, Gather. Writers of all genre and levels, photographers and those just looking to earn free gift cards hang out at these sites and share, comment and promote. I met some of the best people through Gather. When you need advice, support and a cheer squad, look to those in the same trenches as you.

I admit, when I first joined Gather I didn't see its potential. I posted a few things, looked at my points balance and decided it would take ages for me to get a gift card like that and promptly forgot about it. Later, after I had my blog up and running strong for several months, I decided to start reposting there with the mindset of 'I'm going to write them anyways, I may as well try to earn something for my effort'. Little did I know how valuable Gather would turn out to be.

I had belonged to writer sites before, namely Themestream back in the early 90s, but never got too seriously involved in any of the communities. Reposting to Gather would bring up my blog traffic and earned me my first regular blog readers outside of my friends and family circle. I got feedback, answers to my questions and later, a growing social network family.

There are a number of sites like these, and to cover them all would take me a new book (I could call it *Gather While We Mae...*) so I will just suggest that you Google "writer groups" to locate some. They are vital to your social network success. Before you jump in feet first and inundate everyone with long descriptions of all your books' details, you may want to follow my three top tips for success.

1. **Give more than you take.** I believe in karma, reaping and sowing and you get what you put in. If you charge into a group of people demanding that everyone come follow your blog and hit the like button on your book page, you will probably get little response. Amazingly enough, this happens far too often in both marketing and life. In the words of Martin Luther King, "Any man can be great, because any man can serve."

2. **Make sure you can be found.** Amazingly enough, I often find that as I search through someone's profile to find their blog, there's no mention.

Your blog, book, or whatever you are trying to promote, should be listed prominently and often. I don't mean spam it down everyone's throats, but if there's a place to leave a few words about yourself, they shouldn't be "I luvz kittenz". You can have that, but add "and you can see mine on my blog - kittenz.com" Make it easy for people to find you.

3. **Leave the ego.** If you are rich and famous, you have earned your ego. Until then, we're all in the same boat and none of us can afford to play the snoot. No one likes the snoot, no one helps him and he is very lonely and usually never very successful. Go back to what Martin Luther King says in my tip #1. When you serve others, you are great, even if you never get your book in a store, you will still be great.

21

Data Analyzers: Using Facts to Sell Your Fiction

As an author, having a marketing plan is essential to earning money from your books. It's not enough to rely on your perceptions, as this can lead to flimsy publishing plans that fall apart in the face of unforeseen events. Instead, you need to base your plans on data, specifically on the numbers that come from your book sales.

You need to know how much money you're making, where your sales are coming from, and which books are selling the best. An easy way to gather this data is to use a data analyzer such as Book Report (getbookreport.com) or BookTrakr (booktrakr.com). These tools gather sales information for all your books and organize the information for you.

Once you have this data, you can use it to make more informed decisions about your publishing plans. For example, if you see that a significant percentage of your sales are coming from a particular country, you might consider investing in translations to appeal to a new set of readers. If you see that one of your forgotten titles is suddenly surging in sales, you can adjust your plans to promote it and release a sequel.

With this data in hand, you can build a detailed and data-driven publishing plan. This should include target dates for publishing new books, as well as dates for starting promotions through various channels such as Goodreads,

Facebook, Twitter, and Instagram.

By basing your plans on data, you can avoid wasting money on ideas that aren't likely to pay off, and focus your efforts on the areas that are most likely to generate sales. And by tracking your sales data over time, you can continue to refine your plans and make better decisions in the future.

This benefited me most recently when I saw a sales spike in one of my forgotten titles for kids. With zero promotion, *The Christmas Spiders* surges to 38% of my total sales every December. Now that I know, I'll build that into my plans and schedule some promotion, audio book version and a follow up book. I always knew that I sold some copies of that book each holiday. I just didn't realize how significant they were.

Picking a data analyzer depends on your situation. If you have most or all of your books available on Amazon, you can use Book Report to track that information for you. Book Report gathers sales information for all your books, including extended channels. You can check sales by book, country, your top sellers in easy to read charts. Best part is that Book Report is free until you make $1,000 a month on KDP, and then it costs $19 a month. When I'm bringing in $1k a month from book royalties, I will happily pay Book Report to count it all for me.

BookTrakr (booktrakr.com) is better for authors who publish wide including Draft2Digital and Smashwords. BookTrakr doesn't have a free version like Book Report, but the cost is from .99 to $19.99 based on how many books you have. BookTrakr and Book Report both have free trials so you can check them out before committing.

In short, if you want to earn a living as an author, you need to be a professional and keep track of your numbers. Use a data analyzer to gather this information, and then use it to build a detailed and data-driven publishing plan. With a little focus and effort, you can turn your hopes into reality and build a profitable career as an author.

Originally published as "Data Analyzers: Using Facts to Sell Your Fiction." FundsforWriters, September 16, 2023. https://fundsforwriters.com/data-analyzers-using-facts-to-sell-your-fiction/

22

Final Word on Marketing

Great marketing won't sell a bad book, but a good book won't sell *without* great marketing. Selling your book to the people you interact with is nothing to be ashamed of. If you had a new car, you'd show it off. We plaster our kids' latest photos across the vision of anyone we come across. Why do we then work like donkeys to get our dream book finished and available, and then never share it?

As I was working on this book I attended all the author chats I could with other authors and asked the same question; what are you doing to market your story? The typical answer was; I haven't really. No one gave me an actual plan. A few times my question was actually bypassed and left unanswered.

This is your baby, and if you can't love it no one else will. You have to be your biggest fan. I'm not saying to cram your book down everyone's throats until they dread seeing your approach. I'm saying, when there is an opportunity to share, do it.

A marketing campaign is like trying to walk on snow. If you try to walk over the top of a deep drift in your regular snow boots you won't get very far before you crash through the delicate frozen crust and are left to struggle the rest of the way.

Your marketing plan should be like snowshoes, spread wide to reduce too much stress in any one area. If you have mentions of your book across Facebook, Twitter, Linkd In, Flickr, various blogs, Goodreads... etc. etc. no one can get overwhelmed with your mentions.

As a creative spirit you will find new ways to use this information that will take into account your own tastes and talents. I encourage you to explore these ideas and build upon them. You are limited by your imagination and your attitude. Expect mistakes, but look at them as opportunities instead of fails. Accidents are just great ideas you don't recognize yet. Now go bring your new baby to the world. All you need is like!

III

A Few Tools

To end this, I pass on a few helpful tools from my personal journey. Binaural beats are a non evasive tested way to hack the brain into productivity. How to get 15,000 publishable words written in three days, hush the imposter syndrome and how write a press release are also here. As I find new tips, I share them in my weekly newsletter, Authortunities, which is free to read at authortunities.substack.com.

Much of this was compiled from workshops I've taught. I hope you find it useful.

23

A Recap: The Top 5 Tips for Building Story

Everyone has their own approach to creating story and every approach that produces writing is valid. The act of creating a peopled world from imagination is nothing short of miraculous. The old adage about size not mattering is absolutely true. Whether you are writing a flash or an epic, the same principles apply.

While writing is hardly a one-size-fits all undertaking, every author has something that made a big difference in their career. Here are five of the things I've learned that have helped me the most:

1. **Know the why before you try.** Anyone who thinks the *why* they write doesn't matter is doing themselves an injustice. The *why* is at the heart of everything and can be the difference between fulfillment or frustration. When you know *why* you want to write it helps you understand *what* to write, *where* to release it and for *who*. Knowing *why* you want to write helps you to streamline your career and avoid a terrible moment of realizing you just spent a good deal of time and energy on something that will not get you where you need to go.

2. **You are the secret plot twist.** The best advice I ever got as a writer

was from Bryan Thao Worra. Up until that point my stories were all what I *thought* readers wanted because I'd read these types of stories hundreds of times. Bryan suggested I add my personal quirks into my work instead of writing rehashed regurgitations of what I had read before. Adding my authentic experience was a game changer and I've sold everything I've written since and even won a few awards for it.

3. **Timeless stories change readers.** Not every story has to change the world, but the ones that do last generations. The best way to retain relevance is to make your work matter. If you could say something to change the world, what would that be? Now add that message into your work. Think back to the stories that have stayed with you. More than likely they changed you somehow. We entertain, but we can also teach, open minds and inspire. Our readers will return the love by remembering us long after that final page turns.

4. **Hurting heroes, happy readers.** As kind as we are to our readers, we have to be cruel to our characters. One of the reasons people read story is to escape and see problems solved. We don't read a story to know that everything is fine. Let your characters out of one sticky situation by breaking something else. Protagonists must suffer or they won't engage. What works in the gym also works on the page: no pain, no gain.

5. **Get it right from the beginning.** As boring as it may seem, formatting your work before the first sentence goes down can save you a lot of trouble later. I have a template in my Google Drive already formatted in Shunn so all I have to do is start typing. Since this is how most publishers want to see a submitted manuscript, I'm ahead of the game. Shunn formatting makes my work easy to read, which is why publishers ask for it this way. As a side benefit, it also makes it easier to write. You can find Shunn formatting at https://www.shunn.net/format/classic/.

These things aren't the end-all secrets to fast fame and fortune. If you discover that formula please share! Until then, I hope this gives you a boost toward your success.

A RECAP: THE TOP 5 TIPS FOR BUILDING STORY

Originally publishing in Horror Writers Association newsletter February 2022.

24

Taming Impostor Shadow

I don't believe in Impostor Syndrome. A *syndrome* suggests an affliction, something wrong with me, something beyond my control. That framing never felt accurate. I use the term *impostor shadow* instead.

A shadow only appears when something stands in the light. The larger the shadow, the brighter the source. In that sense, self-doubt is not evidence of fraudulence. It is evidence that I am stepping into something visible. The impostor shadow grows in proportion to my courage. What we call impostor syndrome is often the natural tension that comes with growth. It is the mind recalibrating to a new level of exposure.

Whatever name we give it, nearly every writer encounters this moment, whether new to the craft or seasoned by years of publication. It's that flash of panic when we are certain we are a complete charlatan and about to be exposed.

Here's the good news: we are in very good company.

Great writers have all experienced this crippling psychological pattern at some point. John Steinbeck once said, "I am not a writer. I've been fooling myself and other people." I think we all feel that way at some point, but because impostor syndrome occurs primarily among high achievers, the doubt you feel is actually a reassurance that you do deserve your successes. Good writers are often unable to internalize and accept their accomplishments, giving credit to luck instead.

I love this story Neil Gaiman tells of facing his own impostor.

"Some years ago, I was lucky enough to be invited to a gathering of great and good people: artists and scientists, writers and discoverers of things. And I felt that at any moment they would realize that I didn't qualify to be there, among these people who had really done things. On my second or third night there, I was standing at the back of the hall, while a musical entertainment happened, and I started talking to a very nice, polite, elderly gentleman about several things, including our shared first name. And then he pointed to the hall of people, and said words to the effect of, 'I just look at all these people, and I think, what the heck am I doing here? They've made amazing things. I just went where I was sent.'

And I said, 'Yes. But you were the first man on the moon. I think that counts for something.'

And I felt a bit better. Because if Neil Armstrong felt like an impostor, maybe everyone did. Maybe there weren't any grown-ups, only people who had worked hard and also got lucky and were slightly out of their depth, all of us doing the best job we could, which is all we can really hope for."

Maya Angelou once confessed "I have written 11 books but each time I think 'Uh-oh, they're going to find out now. I've run a game on everybody, and they're going to find me out.'" Personally, I feel this way every time I get a compliment on my work. I have a checklist that I run down in my head to smother the urge to confess my lack of talent.

1. Did I plagiarize the thing I'm being complimented on? If yes, then confess to my crime. If no, then say thank you.
2. Do I have to be perfect? If yes, then give up now while I'm behind. If no, then say thank you.
3. Is the guilt I feel internally going to physically cause me harm? If yes, quit now and preserve what I have left of my health. If no, then say thank you.

If the immortal icons of literary achievement like Gaiman, Angelou and Steinbeck sometimes feel like frauds, who are we to fight this natural byproduct of being a creative? In my years as an editor I have learned that when someone tells me their work is the best thing since sliced bread, it probably isn't and for every writer that apologizes as I prepare to look over their work, I'm probably in for a treat.

I wish I had a cure for this terrible feeling. It's a bitter irony that the artist often doesn't get to enjoy their creation to the fullest. We see every typo, instance of passive voice and brush stroke. Good artists create in spite of the constant nagging self-doubt. Great artists embrace it.

Seems like an easy concept to grasp, but good luck remembering it at midnight when facing a blank screen and mind. Every time you hear that inner voice whisper that you are a fraud, know that you are in the company of the best. What you are creating is a threat or there would be no reason for self-doubt. Allow yourself a moment of guilty pride before the Fraud Police lock you down...

Then get back to work and make something even better. Like Tennessee Williams said, "What's talent but the ability to get away with something?"

Originally published in January 2022 Horror Writers Association newsletter.

25

Binaural Beats for Focus

Deadline approaches, and the screen is blank. You place your fingers on the keyboard, but your mind is also blank. All you can think of is another coffee and the laundry that waits. Where is the muse? The third email has just popped in your inbox asking for a sneak peek at the painting you've been commissioned to do. You glance at the photograph of the beloved pet you're supposed to immortalize and then back at the canvas. So far all you've managed to capture is a lot of nothing. Where is the muse?

You have three chords set, but hardly enough to put all the words you've been given to music. You strum aimlessly as you stare out the window. Nothing is coming except the mail, which proves to be just enough distraction to pull you away for a few hours. Where is the muse?

Know that you're not alone in these moments. All creatives at one time or another have experienced a lack of production due to an absence of ideas. It's a frustrating, humiliating experience to have the opportunity but not the creative energy to take advantage of it.

Reasons for blocked creativity can range from the physical and metaphysical to the emotional and spiritual. For every reason we have to create, there seems to be five reasons to put it off. From the mundane day-to-day tasks that require our attention to deep rooted emotional damage, anything that keeps us from expressing ourselves creatively can be detrimental to our growth. It's vital for our well being to overcome obstacles and create in spite of it all.

Emotional roadblocks are a leading cause of creative distress. Before I learned to identify and overcome these energy sappers I sometimes found myself one sentence into an article I needed to finish with no words to fill the page. Fortunately, there are many ways to get through your creative blocks and move on. Once you have found a few effective ways to woo your muse, you'll find yourself achieving more than you ever thought possible.

Hypnotherapy, counseling and meditation have all helped me to overcome emotional blockages, but I find personal meditation to be the most effective in removing creative hurdles. It's also the easiest, requiring no appointments or preparation. After a meditative session I always find that I can identify why I was unable to continue a project and move beyond it.

I've found binaural beat compositions to be particularly helpful when meditating for creativity. Binaural music is an auditory illusion created when two similar frequencies of sound are played into each ear. Our brain perceives the two similar frequencies as pulses, or beats.

The superior olivary complex, located in the brain stem, is the part of our brain that identifies the direction of sound. When it perceives two similar frequencies, it responds by synchronizing neural activity. This synchronization is called entrainment.

Simply put, when the brain hears certain binaural frequencies it realigns and smooths the path for all synapses to start firing in a synchronized fashion. The type of binaural beat you listen to depends on what activity you seek to synchronize. There are four different types of brain waves that we understand:

- **Delta Waves** are associated with deep sleep, meditation, astral projection and healing.
- **Theta Waves** are associated with dreaming, accessing the subconscious, intuition and creativity.
- **Alpha Waves** are the conscious mind at rest. Alphas are associated with coordinating, categorizing and calculations.
- **Beta Waves** are the next step up and are associated with active thinking,

complex problem solving and excitement.
- **Gamma Waves**, a fifth type, are still not entirely understood. General thought is that they link the different functions of the brain and are involved in self awareness and spirituality.

To align your creativity and bring it into hyper drive, binaural beats that activate the Theta Waves are the most beneficial. To use them, all you need is a set of headphones, a place to be comfortable and 15-30 minutes.

Simply select your binaural beat composition and how you want to listen to it. Put your headphones on, relax and let your brain get a realignment. I have a friend who enjoys a binaural session in the bathtub complete with candles, incense and aromatherapy oils. My sessions are much simpler. I relax in my office chair and simply listen. Since I listen to prep myself for writing, I prefer to be in a position where I can launch straight into work when finished.

A favorite composition of mine is pure binaural beat with no other sounds called "1hr Theta Binaural Beat Session (7hz) ~ Pure" on YouTube. It's a solid hour of Theta enhancing tones. Do use headphones since binaural beats depend on the ear hearing the difference in frequency between the left and the right to be effective.

Binaural beats can be used in conjunction with an established meditation practice or to start one. It's important to have a distraction free time set aside for this this activity as activities that require concentration will distract from it.

This chapter focuses on using binaural beats to enhance creativity, but there are many other reasons to implement this easy therapy into your day, including:

- reducing stress and anxiety
- increasing focus and concentration
- increase motivation and confidence
- deeper meditation

- improving performance
- boosting mood

Find binaural beats for free on YouTube or purchase them from holistic venues that sell audio. Practice a half hour of this everyday before you launch into your creative pursuits and you will find your blocks have become history.

Originally published in Evolving Magazine, May, 2019.

26

Supernatural Productivity Without Selling Your Soul

W hat if there is a way to write more than double your typical daily word count and have time to do all your other projects...? What if you could do it without drugs, magic spells or selling your soul to the nearest productivity demon? I recently stumbled upon this superpower in a moment of desperation—and of course I'm sharing.

Crisis can pave the way for ingenious solutions. Last week I had to write 15k words in four days—almost 4k a day. That's a lot for me. I find 1k words a day pretty easy and 2k is a solid effort. For me, this was going to be a marathon. I made my word count the first three days but I paid the price. My house was a mess, my brain was dead, my inbox exploded and I'm pretty sure I missed a shower or two somewhere. This is a usual state for me when I'm meeting a big deadline. When I reached the last 5,000 words I was exhausted. I had no words left.

That morning I sat down at my computer already tired and discouraged. If I could be doing anything else—including a dental visit—I would have been there. I thought about how many words I can get out easily, even when I'm tired. I decided to write just that—500 words—and then do something else. I made myself a chart with my needed word count divided up into 500 word increments. In between, I added other tasks that desperately needed doing.

My list looked something like this:

- 500 words
- Load of dishes in dishwasher
- 500 words
- Wipe counters
- 500 words
- Vacuum/mop kitchen
- 500 words
- Chop ginger root—make jars of ginger honey tea
- 500 words
- Fix necklace catch
- 500 words

It was hard to stay focused, but I did the first 500 words and went to start the dishes. I returned feeling more motivated. I can get through 500 words, and now my dishes weren't screaming at me. I went through the next set faster so I could get to the counters. 500 words later, and my floors were mopped. My kitchen was clean again, and I had 1,500 words done. I felt like a superhero.

It was rinse and repeat for the rest of the day. I found that walking away to do something else woke me up and gave me time to think about where the story was going. At the same time, knowing the rest of my life wasn't suffering while I was working at my desk energized me. Toward the end I was getting tired so I took a break in my clean kitchen with a cup of honey ginger tea I had made. I went back to my desk feeling like a champion and I smashed the rest out before midnight.

I had a 2k story due the next day, so I tried it again:

- 500 words
- Clean/organize bottom office shelf
- 500 words
- Clean/organize middle office shelf
- 500 words
- Clean/organize top office shelf
- 500 words

The shelves I refer to have been an issue for awhile. Hidden just off screen in all my Zoom calls, they had become a dumping spot for boxes I might want to reuse, books I wanted to read and miscellaneous junk. Every time I wanted to pull out anything useful like printer paper, garbage would fall out on me. The shelves were a pet peeve I kept meaning to get to after the next deadline.

I flew through the first 500 words excited to finally clear out the bottom shelf. I found some things I thought I'd lost. I discovered a stack of prints I'd meant to frame and hang. There was a half packed box I was going to send to my grand kids. I cleared out the junk, made a list for future sprints and went back to the story. I flew through the rest of that story in micro-chunks and cleaned up my hidden shame at the same time. No more would I wait to do projects after deadlines, I decided. These off desk tasks would be part of my deadlines.

I'm sure I'm not the only writer to have tried this, so I won't claim it. I've heard of timed writing sprints but personally it doesn't work for me to race against a clock. I put word count before story when I race. Using the word count itself as my goal was the key for me. When my mind would start wandering, I'd check my word count. Only 323 words left to finish this micro-chunk? Easy-peasy… let me knock that out and I can finally go [insert activity]. As a bonus, I found the emotional boost from accomplishing non-writing tasks energized and motivated me so I was charged up and ready to go. When I finished the story, I didn't feel like I had a bunch of neglected stuff piled up, waiting for me.

I chose 500 word chunks because that's the word count I can easily put out without too much effort. I don't think there is a magic number for this. If you can spit out 1,000 words easily, use that as your goal. If your magic number is 200, don't worry about it. That's the right number for you. Whatever activity you choose as your alternate, start with the things that are screaming for your attention. If your dishes aren't bothering you but writing a card for a friend is, write the card. Maybe the thing screaming at you is something fun like an art project. Then go do that. I think the key is tackling something that will provide a sense of accomplishment and relief.

I've been doing this sprint-task writing all week and by the end of it I've written 7k of fiction, three columns and a poem… I've also taken care of a bunch of small chores so when I turn off my computer I can actually relax.

If you already do this, share what you've learned with me. If you try this for the first time, let me know how it works. At the end of the day, just remember there is no one size fits all trick for productivity. The best method for you is the one that gets your words on the page. If this technique helps you do that, it's a winner—no soul selling required.

Originally published in the Horror Writers Association Newsletter March 2022.

27

The Power of the Press Release

Wish you could find easy, free promotion with major impact on multiple platforms? What if it could even have the potential to reach an international, multi-media audience and go viral? Your wish is granted. Just master the press release.

I've heard people say they don't like to send out a press release because they don't want to impose on busy reporters or look like they're showing off. I worked for years as an editorial assistant and one of my many jobs was to put together the arts and community section of a weekly newspaper. My task was to fill those pages, and it didn't matter with what. I was thrilled whenever I got a well done press release. It meant I had good content ready to publish, which made my job easier. I remembered people who sent me good press releases by name. I guarantee I always opened their emails first.

Besides helping the newspaper, especially in the summer months when content runs thin, you are helping any organization you are involved with. If everyone who recently won a Bram Stoker Award® or other HWA awards sent a press release to their local media outlets, imagine how much coverage and prestige that would bring not only to the HWA, but horror as a genre? Press releases are not a selfish act of personal promotion. You are helping some poor editor fill empty newsprint and most likely sharing the spotlight with your professional affiliations, publishers and co-authors. Being a winner isn't a solo act. Show off your success and you shine on those who helped you get there as well.

Here's a real life, recent example: Following Lee Murray's recent double Stoker win, she knew she needed to send out a press release. She wrote up a beautiful release and then asked if I could look it over. I tried not to cackle too gleefully. Press releases happen to be one of my favorite things. With a few simple tweaks and formatting changes (this time, *don't* use Shunn) she had a PSA any editor would love to see. Within two hours her story was picked up by a major news outlet, and I was thrilled to see they used my exact headline. The entire wording of this news item, down to the photo cutlines, is just about word for word what Lee sent them.

See that news story here: https://creativebop.org.nz/2021/05/kiwi-writer-makes-international-waves-with-prestigious-literary-wins/

A good press release is a gift that benefits both the receiving and sending ends. The idea is to provide a lovely news item of interest so some harried editor can copy and paste. It should have a few good quality photos with it. Ideally a headshot, an action shot (book signing, convention, etc) and a photo of something that goes with the story. A close up of a trophy, your book cover art and anything similar. They probably will only use one, but if they lay out your story and have a pesky inch or two to fill, a nice close up of your front cover is perfect. A few photos gives them some flexibility.

Now for the anatomy of the actual press release. You will want to start with the file names of the photos you're attaching. Please identify your photos properly. It's annoying and it wastes time to rename your headpic.jpg to something an editor can actually find. Paste each file name at the top of your document in a plain, non serif font like Arial. Add the file extension. Don't worry, I'll have an example so you can see how all this looks and it will make sense.

After the image name, you will write what is called a cutline. This should be bolded and directly underneath the image name. This is to describe what the photo is, written as you would read it in a new story. Remember, this is a copypasta gift. Book covers, by the way, usually don't need a cutline. The title identifies it and a cutline is redundant.

Next, write a headline. These have their own, truncated language. Because they are so concise, double meanings, puns and other word play are often used. The idea is to grab attention and justify why it matters. In the case of Lee's: **Kiwi Writer Makes International Waves with Prestigious Literary Wins**.

Dynamic words like *prestigious* and *literary* set the tone and let the reader know this is of importance. Using the phrase "international waves" let's them know this is of global importance. This is no small prize. This is something grand. Using the plural wins signifies multiple awards. It's about a writer (which statistically a majority of the population identifies with), but not just any writer. This one is a "Kiwi." For New Zealanders, that's a mark of pride and worth noting. For everyone else in the world, it's a bit exotic, and therefore interesting.

After the headline, write up a simple but detailed story. The first paragraph is called the nut graph and it means the entire context of the story can be explained in a nutshell paragraph—a nut graph (or also nut graf). This is in a direct who-what-where-when-why format.

First paragraph from Lee's news item:

"In a New Zealand first, Tauranga author Lee Murray won two prestigious Bram Stoker Awards® at an awards event hosted by the Horror Writers Association over the weekend." (creativebop.org.nz)

Who: Tauranga author Lee Murray
  What: won two prestigious Bram Stoker Awards®
  Where: an event hosted by HWA
  When: over the weekend
  Why (this matters): a New Zealand first

Now for the body of your text. Expand on this first paragraph with the proof. This is where it's good to use quotes, both from yourself in third person and others speaking about the topic. "There is nothing wrong with quoting yourself in a press release," says HWA columnist Angela Yuriko Smith. "The press release is written from the media's point-of-view and they appreciate the ready-made quote."

Be brief and write for an 8th grade education. A press release is not where you want world building and purple prose. From 500 to 800 words is a good length. If the news outlet wants more, they will contact you. And this brings us to the next item. Close and contact.

If your press release is for an upcoming event you are publicizing, this is where I like to recap the essential details. Times, dates, ticket price and links should go here in crisp detail. "The next Bram Stoker Awards® banquet will be held at The Curtis Hotel in Denver, Colorado USA from May 12-15, 2022. For more information, visit the Horror Writers Association at horror.org."

And now, your contact details in case the news outlet wants a follow up. "For more information, please contact [Name] at [phone number] or [email]." And that's it. You don't need a cover letter. Don't try to convince the news outlet of how important you are, how much everyone likes your work or who you know. All of that should already be in the press release. All they want to do is glance at your email, download your clearly labeled photos and be one step closer to another deadline done.

Finally, *please* use the subject line of your email. This is a good place to just paste your headline. I like to use the "RE:" but it isn't necessary. Just don't fill this valuable real estate with "Press Release." There may be 500 of those ahead of you that week, and the editor doesn't want to search through any of them.

Here's a sample press release template you can use based on the Lee Murray news item we've been referencing.

Lee_Murray_Headshot.jpg
Lee Murray

Lee_Murray_BramStokers_2019.jpg
Lee Murray at the 2019 Bram Stoker Awards® held 11 May at the Amway Grand Plaza Hotel, Grand Rapids, USA. Photo credit: Ellen

Datlow

Black Cranes_Cover.jpg

Kiwi Writer Makes International Waves with Prestigious Literary Wins
[Nutgraph]

[Body of your press release]

For more information please contact [Name] at [phone number] or [email].
You can also visit [website].

And that's it. You now have all the tools you need to go forth and share your good news with the world. Next month I'll cover press release etiquette, newsworthy topics and how to build your press release contact list. And now, get your press release together and go market your words.

Press Release Etiquette

It's important to remember that we are not the center of *the* universe. Ever. Maybe when we're children, but after we hit the non-adorable puberty stage, we're done. This is especially true with editors. This doesn't mean you aren't important. You are the center of *your* universe, as you should be. Just recognize that the editor you are contacting has their own universe to worry about. Take that into account and you are already way ahead.

So when you send a press release, be polite and considerate. Submit your piece in plenty of time if you'd like it to be published by a certain date, and if it doesn't make that date definitely don't call the editor angry about it. If your piece gets in by that date, send a quick thank you note or even a token gift of appreciation. They just gave you hundreds of dollars of free promotion. If your press release doesn't have a 'publish by' date, then watch for it and when you see it publish, send that thank you note (an email is fine). You can set Google alerts up for yourself if you have a lot of press releases going out online.

(How to set up a Google Alert: https://support.google.com/websearch/answ er/4815696?hl=en)

In my experience, there is nothing wrong with sending a brief message to make sure they received your press release fine and if they needed any follow up. Editors get a lot of material across their desk and are generally happy when people are politely proactive about their submission.

If for some reason it doesn't get used after a few months, don't take it personally. At a small town weekly newspaper I would receive from up to 500 press releases in a week. I could usually squeeze in about 5-10 a week. I encourage you to send a follow up message saying you are disappointed it didn't get to run but you understand the editor's limitations and you appreciate the privilege of submission. This sentiment will get you very far.

You can also ask if your submission was formatted to their preference and invite them to share their preferences, but please don't ask for a critique. If they have the time, they will almost always be glad to give you pointers. That's helping you to help them. The editor wants your press release. You are doing them a favor by sending high quality, free content. They are doing you a favor if they print it. There are just a lot of people asking for favors. Lucky for us, most are asking badly.

MAKE YOURSELF RELEVANT

A common mistake I've seen with press releases, like publishing in general, is sending to the wrong market. Don't send your press release about your literary win to your local sports news. But, if your book has anything to do with sports they are an excellent place to send it… as long as you let them know there is a connection there.

Your local newspaper has an interest—an angle—in you no matter what you are doing because you are local. Local people are of local interest. Your state-wide publications often have the same interest. That's why so many headlines start off by identifying where someone comes from. No one knows who Joe Smith is, but "Missouri Man Bites Snake" might be their neighbor. Everyone in Missouri knows a man from Missouri.

The trick is finding connections. Put yourself in the editor's POV and think about their needs. A sports editor needs anything related to sports. A small town publication wants to know your connection to the small town. If your town is famous for ghost tours, news of your story in a ghost themed anthology is perfect. If it's late August or September, your ghost themed anthology is newsworthy anywhere Halloween is celebrated. If it's April, and your town or publication isn't known for ghosts... find a different relatable angle.

JUST DO IT

In the end, the best press release is the one you actually send. Even the worst releases get published by editors desperate to fill space. It costs you nothing but time, and the potential reward is free, high value promotion. As long as you approach an editor (or anyone) with respect and appreciation and follow the simple steps I've outlined in this column, you have a good chance of becoming a favorite.

This chapter was originally published in the Horror Writer Association's newsletter, June and July 2021.

28

Be an Authortunist

B e opportunistic. I can't stress enough how you need to be an outside the box thinking opportunistic maniac to make this work. The key that you look for is involvement. If you have any way to interact, do it. Recently I saw on a monthly newsletter from Goodreads that they were having a contest. To enter, you had to create a PowerPoint style slideshow to tell a story.

I looked at that contest like everyone else, but where the majority of them looked at the prize I looked at what could it be about. Could it be a tool for me to market my own stuff? I read the magic words "can be about anything" and I scribbled it and the due date on my To Do list. This was now a marketing tool. Then I looked at the prize, out of curiosity. It didn't matter to me if I won or not. The prize could have been a bag of manure for all I cared; the important thing was that I could use it as a tool.

So I made my story. Marketing that feeds into more marketing is the most powerful, so I wanted to do more than just talk about *End of Mae*. I wanted to also introduce the fact that I was writing a book, this one, about the other story. It hit me that making a story about the story behind the story would make an interesting hook, so I called it *The Story Behind the Story*. My contest entry was serving the purpose to sell my fictional book, introduce and generate excitement for my nonfiction book, and provide another marketing experiment that I could write about in that same book.

Because it was a 'story' I gave my book the tone of a fairy tale. It starts out with the words, "Once upon a time a writer decided to write her first book. You can see that the imagery is fantastical and has a distinct feel of magic. I proceeded to tell the story of how I wrote the book, and then detailed my Second Life marketing campaign in a story telling tone.

I had opportunities to cross promote Second Life and bloggers that had published a review on me by adding buttons that linked to their reviews of *End of Mae* on their blogs. Because I used Second Life, and promoted other bloggers, it was appropriate for me to share this with all the parties. I also shared it with the avatars whose photos were included in the story. Because I wasn't actually trying to win, but promote, I could relax and not feel competitive. This contest entry allowed me to directly promote my two books, one not even written yet to:

- Second Life on Facebook and its 174,000 and climbing members
- Promote the bloggers who had reviewed
- Communicate that I reciprocate promotion
- My blog readers when I posted it in the sidebar and posted
- Goodreads, my Amazon Author Page and everywhere that autoposts
- Visitors to the End of Mae Virtual Visitor's Center because I posted a slideshow directly in the Welcome Area
- My Facebook, Twitter and LinkdIn
- Slideshare users, which was a new group for me. I had 48 views in the first 20 minutes.
- The Goodreads group that would be judging all the slideshow entries, and if I made it into the top 5, the author herself.
- If I won, that was just icing on the cake as I could promote that I'd won, not to mention an actual prize.

If I had asked Second Life and Goodreads could they please promote a slideshow about my books were, they would have refused. The contest was my excuse, my license to promote. These are the opportunities that you have to be greedy for. It's a win-win for all parties. Everyone gets promotion.

I promoted Second Life to Goodreads people, and Goodreads people to Second Life, not to mention the bloggers and friends mentioned. Toward the end that little slideshow had nearly 5,000 viewers, and I added narration and posted it on YouTube.

FREE BOOKS

The face of the literary world is changing rapidly for authors with the advancing wave of technology. Traditional paper publications are being edged out by faster, cheaper and more ecological digital publications. Electronic books are interactive and cost very little, if anything, to produce. Every author should be dipping in to this market.

Don't think you have the technical chops to lay out an ebook? Thanks to Reedsy.com, anyone can lay out a very nice ebook and print in no time at all. Since discovering it I've put together and published 12 ebooks. Reedsy has a small note and a link in the front matter to promote their site, and if you tag @ReedsyHQ! on Twitter/X you get even more cooperative promotion. I have professional layout artists for both *Space and Time* magazine and Yuriko Publishing. I still plan on using Reedsy for many of my own books and projects. Layout options are limited, but Reedsy builds some of the nicest ebooks I've seen in no time at all. Check out the front matter of this book to try it for yourself.

Many people still use Smashwords to send out free copies to reviewers and friends. When I did my live Q&A sessions on Goodreads I offered a free ebook from Smashwords to everyone that attended. This may have come across as generous, but that wasn't why I did it. I did it to generate reviews.

Bookfunnel is also fantastic for this and they have a number of features like direct sales, audiobook sales and readers can access their downloads in a free app.

Goodreads has a great community of writers and bloggers. These are the people you want to get into your book and fall in love with it. They get typically get requests to review books all the time, and often have a list of books they are catching up with. When they have gotten to interact with the author, they are at their most interested. This is your standing out from the crowd moment. Use you spotlight wisely and romance all attendees, and then, in the first moments of new romance hit them up with commitment by giving them your book.

I couldn't have been so generous if I only had access to paperback copies. I gave away two paperbacks in the first month, and each one was around $10 to buy and ship. I gave away around 50 plus Smashword books in the Goodreads chats and it cost me nothing.

Quite the opposite, I was paid back in heaps of promotional value. Some of the chat attendees reviewed it, and an even larger number shared my information with everyone in their social networks. Whenever I come across a review blog that I like, I can ask them to review my work and offer them the free version if they are interested.

The other thing that is wonderful about electronic books is the interactive capabilities. As of this publication date these features are unavailable with the Smashwords technology, but I'm sure that will quickly be remedied. The Kindle version, however, available only on amazon.com has a wonderful 'share' function. If you are an author I strongly advise you to get a Kindle over other ereaders based on this function alone.

This enables me, with a few simple actions, to share any passage I happen to be reading on my Facebook and Twitter accounts. What a powerful tool that I have yet to see used by anyone else. It posts automatically, and not only gives the quote that you've selected, but allows you to share a few words also.

I do this occasionally with my own book to share my favorite passages and create buzz. I do it with other author books for the same reason. If you have a Kindle, you should have it set up to connect with your social sites and be sharing at least once a week. I started a daily post of "What I'm Reading Now..." as a way to spark conversation and interact with potential readers. Sometimes it's my own book, but more often than not I share what I am actually reading.

The publishing landscape is reforming the publishing scene in a big way. Artificial intelligence, audiobooks, Text To Speech and the wide adoption of using phones as ereaders has changed the writer landscape beyond recognition from what it was a decade ago. The best mindset we can have for success is a flexible one. Evolution happens.

For Authors: Authortunities

Authortunities is a weekly calendar newsletter designed specifically for writers to find all the author opportunities they need in a single, curated format. Open submission calls, contests, workshops, open mics, grants and more, in your inbox every Saturday.

Organized by emoji, *Authortunities* contains four weeks of valuable opportunities for authors. Enjoy the next two weeks of opportunities at no cost. Access the entire four weeks of opportunities for just $5.55 a month.

However you take advantage of it, your *Authortunities* are waiting for you.

https://authortunities.substack.com/freemonth
Exercise your writes. Get published. Make change.

Did you enjoy this book?

Word-of-mouth recommendations and online reviews are critical to the success of any book. If you enjoyed this book, please tell your friends about it and consider leaving a review at your favorite book seller or library's website.

About the Author

Angela Yuriko Smith is a two-time Bram Stoker Award–winning author, former president of the Horror Writers Association, and publisher of *Space and Time*. As a publishing consultant and coach, she helps writers build sustainable creative careers rooted in art, not arson. She writes *Authortunities* on Substack.

You can connect with me on:
- https://angelaysmith.com
- https://twitter.com/AngelaYSmith
- https://www.facebook.com/Angela.Yuriko.Smiths

Subscribe to my newsletter:
- https://authortunities.substack.com

www.ingramcontent.com/pod-product-compliance
Lightning Source LLC
Chambersburg PA
CBHW060800050426
42449CB00008B/1460